D1412389

# GAUTAMA BUDDHA
## In Life and Legend

*by Betty Kelen*

❂ ❂ ❂

# GAUTAMA BUDDHA
## In Life and Legend

*Lothrop, Lee & Shepard Co., Inc.*

NEW YORK

TO JULI
and her friends, this tale of a man who said:

*"Make what is right become. It is possible to make
what is right become. Were it not possible to
make what is right become, I would not say, 'Make
what is right become.' But because it is possible,
therefore I say, 'Make what is right become.'"*

# Acknowledgement

I wish to thank Mr. M. R. Tongnoi Tongyai, Second Secretary of the Permanent Mission of Thailand to the United Nations, who kindly read my manuscript from a Buddhist's point of view, and gave me the benefit of his comments.

# Foreword

*Brahmin, I lay no wood for fires on altars. Only within burneth the flame I kindle.*

SAMYUTTA-NIKAYA

Gautama Buddha lived twenty-five hundred years ago. Anyone who wishes to know what sort of man he was must peer at him through shrouds of time and thickets of legend. Many of the stories that have been preserved for us appear to tell the life and work of a real man; others are symbolic of the religious beliefs of the Buddhists and the Hindus; others are pure folklore, as old as man and lively with marvels and miracles.

The real miracle is this: that wisdom exists. It is inbuilt in the foundation of the mind, and though it is hardly noticed by ordinary people in their hurry to get on with their everyday affairs, there have been some extraordinary men who have noticed it. They have seen the shape of pure wisdom and have described it in simple language for the rest of us to build our lives upon.

Siddhartha Gautama was one of these gifted men. The moral law he devised became the inspiration of many eastern civilizations, and people ended by assuming that he must have been not a man, but a god. His life story, therefore, like that of other religious teachers, is a sort of sacred drama, the biography of a spirit as well as that of a person.

Gautama's spirit is versatile. It leads through rich jungles of oriental folklore toward the Himalayan ranges of man's thought.

# Contents

# In the Beginning...

*Many a birth have I traversed, seeking the Builder.*

DHAMMAPADA

Religion is man's contact with the mysteries of the infinite, and that is why most religions have tales to tell about the beginnings and ends of things, the limitless past and the unmeasured future. The Buddhist legend-makers have imagined that mankind has existed through aeons of time, each aeon being a number of years so high that no mathematician of earth or heaven can possibly calculate it: twenty-seven zeros after ten might be a modest estimate.

Now and again in this fantastic stream of time, there arises a Buddha—an "Enlightened One"—and he becomes a teacher of his fellow man. Every one of the Buddhas teaches the same thing. When mankind forgets his teaching, it is time for a new Buddha to be born and a new Buddha-age to begin.

We are living today in the age of Gautama Buddha, but we are told that six Buddhas lived before him; some legends count twenty-four or even one hundred, and there are those that speak extravagantly of several hundred million Buddhas who walked the earth before Gautama.

Buddhas are not gods. They are human beings, no different in essence and origin from you and me: sparks of energy bound, according to Buddhist belief, upon the ever-turning Wheel of Life, and every Buddha is fated to be born and reborn throughout an eternity in many different conditions, high and low. In the beginning perhaps he is simply dumb matter, a lump of clay or a rock. After crossing an immense desert of years, his life-spark passes into plants and then animals, and it lives, dies, and is recreated through aeons until at last it animates a man. Birth, decay, old age, death: the Buddha knows this universal cycle scores, even hundreds, of times, as indeed we all do. So far, a Buddha is Everyman.

But there is one respect in which a Buddha differs from others. At some time or another in his myriad lives he has been filled with a sublime determination: to make his soul perfect. From this moment, he is no longer a common man: he is a Bodhisattva—one who is going to be enlightened.

The story of Gautama Buddha, therefore, begins not on earth but in the jeweled and perfumed gardens of the Heaven of Delight, where enthroned in the light of a million suns, a Perfect Being sits meditating upon his long course of lives, like an accomplished actor remembering his past roles.

Once at an inexpressibly remote time he had been a conceited young divinity student named Megha who, after spending some years in the mountains reciting his scriptures and prayers until he knew them by heart, descended into a village of the plains to find it festively arrayed with banners and flowers. His first thought was that these decorations had probably been put out in his honor, but a young girl quickly robbed him of this pleasant idea. "We are holding a festival of welcome for Dipankara Buddha," she told him. "He is going to pass through our village today."

In her hand she held seven lotus flowers which she said she intended to throw beneath the feet of the famous Teacher. Megha persuaded her to sell him five of them.

He joined the throng on the highway and watched the Buddha approach, majestic and benign, his visage calm as a smooth lake. The people hailed him with delight and bowed with their palms pressed together, and the girls ran around him strewing their flowers. The Buddha drew near, and Megha tossed his lotuses; but to his utter amazement, instead of falling onto the path, they remained suspended in the air in a circular pattern, and Dipankara was turning his wonderful gaze upon him.

Megha thrilled throughout his body. Under that glance his vanity fled, and he fell to the ground with his long hair spread so that the Buddha might walk over it.

Dipankara passed on in silence; and yet in thought he had spoken to Megha. The young man felt a wish and a will arise in him: he would forge himself into a Perfect Being, like Dipankara. Fast on that thought came another, the incredible realization that it was actually going to happen; that Dipankara had in fact recognized him as a future Buddha, an Enlightened One.

Now, sitting in the gardens of the Heaven of Delight, he knew that the long discipline was almost complete. The imperfect soul that had once lent life to a divinity student had changed beyond recognition. It had become a Bodhisattva, a Buddha-to-be, with only one life left to live—that of a Teacher.

The Bodhisattva's mind embraced the earth in time and space. He chose the year, the place, the parents; and then he prepared himself for the adventure of rebirth.

# 1

## *The Birth of Buddha*

*It is the rule that when the Bodhisattva ceases to
belong to the hosts of the Heaven of Delight
and enters a mother's womb, an infinite and
splendid radiance passing the glory of the gods is made
manifest throughout the world.*

DIGHA-NIKAYA

Twenty-five centuries ago there flourished in India a
city called Kapilavastu. It lay about a hundred miles
north of the modern city of Benares at the very border of
Nepal where the fertile fields of the Ganges Valley begin
to rise into hills and purple mountains; and beyond, the
land soars to the eternal snows of the Himalayas where
the gods live and the sacred rivers have their source.

The city and the little kingdom that lay around it for
about nine hundred square miles were dominated by a
people of the Sakya Clan. They were Hindus, descendants
of the Aryans, those poetic conquerors who moved into
northern India about 3000 B.C., speaking the mother of
languages, Sanskrit, and compiling the oldest books in
the world, the Vedas. The Aryans were an extraordinary

race of intellectuals who must have made themselves the masters of the more primitive peoples of northern India as much by their brilliant conversation as by force of arms. They had a noble conception of God. "That which exists is One," they said, "though the wise call It by many names."

As the centuries passed, gods galore made their appearance in the skies of India, but it was only the wise who remembered they were but shadows of the One. The Sakyas, a simple farming folk, worshiped numerous painted images with piercing eyes and wondrous black mustaches, and priests were kept busy caring for their temples and shrines and making complicated, costly sacrifices of gold and grain, the flesh of animals, and the intoxicating wine called *soma*.

The Sakyas had a king whom legend tells us was called Suddhodana Gautama. Gautama was his family name, and Suddhodana means "Pure Rice." Various of his noble relatives are said to have been named "White Rice," "Fine Rice," "Washed Rice," and "Immortal Rice"; we may infer that the Sakyas were extremely fond of rice and grew a lot of it.

Suddhodana was deeply in love with his wife, a lady so beautiful that those who saw her could hardly believe their eyes. Her name was Maya, which means Illusion, and they said that it fitted her, for she looked like a girl in a dream. Moreover, she possessed the highest and choicest gifts of intelligence and piety: we are told that she abhorred murder, stealing, lying, immodest behavior, and strong drinks. The only shadow in Maya's life was that she yearned for a child, and she spent a great deal of time visiting temples and praying that a son and heir might be bestowed upon her.

There came the time of the Festival of the Full Moon of Midsummer when the people of Kapilavastu swarmed in the streets, singing and blowing horns. The ankle bells of dancing girls were heard on all sides as their skirts unfurled in colors and spangles, and the sacred cows ran with the crowds, trailing long garlands of flowers from their horns.

Queen Maya enjoyed these festivities for seven days. On the seventh day she rose early, bathed in scented water, and having adorned herself, she went into the city where she distributed the stupendous sum of four hundred thousand gold pieces in alms to the poor. Then she retired to her rooms, lay down upon her bed, and slept.

She dreamed that the great Kings of the Four Quarters, of the North, South, East, and West, came and stood at the four corners of her bed. They raised her, bed and all, and bore her as if on a magic carpet out of the palace, over the roofs of the city, across the rising hills toward the most secret fastnesses of the Himalayas. There they set her down beside a sacred lake, where their four queens were waiting. These heavenly ladies washed Maya in the lake, anointed her with the perfumes of paradise, robed her in clothing of astonishing beauty, and threw garlands about her neck. They led her to a golden mansion built on a silver mountainside, and they made her lie down upon a bed on a veranda overlooking a mountain bathed in golden light.

Not one word of explanation had been given Maya by

the dream-people for their surprising actions; and those caught in a dream ask no questions. Now, as Maya stared entranced at the sublime mountain, she saw appear upon its summit a white elephant. In its trunk, which was like a silver rope, it held a white lotus, and it was descending the mountain at a tremendous speed, yet moving with the ponderous grace and dignity of elephants. As it drew close to the silver mountain and approached the golden palace, the sound of its cries crashed among the peaks, and it came thundering upon the veranda with a grand sound of trumpets, straight toward the paralyzed queen. But it did not harm her. It swerved aside and raced three times around her bed. Only after the third round did it suddenly halt, and then it struck her once with its trunk on her right side and disappeared.

But Maya knew what had become of it. It had entered her womb.

Maya awoke. Oddly enough, she had no feeling of fear left over from her dream; on the contrary, she felt filled with blessed happiness, vitality, and joy. Still, she knew that dreams can have hidden meanings, and she thought she had better tell her husband about it. She therefore went with her ladies to the palace gardens where there was a shady grove of asoka trees, while a servant was sent to request King Suddhodana to meet her there.

The king was sitting in judgment upon his throne, surrounded by councilors and courtiers, but upon receiving the queen's message, he left them, and coming to the grove, asked her why she had disturbed his important business. Maya then related to him her dream, and when she came to the part about the elephant, she said, "It was like unto snow and silver, exceeding the glory of the sun and moon, with stately pace and well-built, with six tusks, and noble, his limbs as firm as diamonds and full of beauty—a splendid elephant!"

And Maya asked her husband, "What do you think it means?"

King Suddhodana did not know what it meant, but he thought it might be wise to find out, especially when Maya began to worry that there might be some evil omen lurking in it. He summoned his Brahmins, his priests and soothsayers, the wise men of his court. They came in their white togas, their topknots gleaming with oil and the sacred cords slanting across their breasts, and they stood as still as bronze statues as they listened to Maya and weighed her words. When she had finished, they gave their interpretation.

"This dream brings no misfortune to your race," they said, "but a great joy. For a son will be born to you, a worthy descendant of the royal Sakyas. If he dwells in a house, he will become a king, a Universal Monarch, and rule the world. But if he should choose to leave his house, to forsake royal power, and go forth among mankind, out of compassion, then he will become a Buddha, and the wisest of men."

The king then treated his Brahmins to fine foods and rewarded them with gifts. Their words had filled him with joy and relief, for like anyone who tries to run a country, his head was bursting with more problems than it could hold, and what he wanted most was a brilliant son who would solve them all for him.

In the months that followed, Maya lived in happiness,

vital and unwearied, protected from every ill by watchful, invisible gods. When she thought the time had come when she would give birth, she reminded Suddhodana that it was the custom of the women of her family to have their babies under the parental roof. Suddhodana therefore gave his wife permission to travel to her native city, Devadaha, some miles away. He sent out an army of servants to smooth down the road along which she would pass; and lest she should grow tired of looking at the eternal snows of the Himalayas, he commanded potted plants to be set up on both sides of the road. As we shall see, King Suddhodana was not a man who did things by halves.

Maya set out in a palanquin with a company of servants and ladies-in-waiting. When they had traveled for about twenty-four miles to the very edge of her native land, the queen, looking past the potted plants, saw a lovely wooded dell known as the Lumbini Grove, full of giant trees and shrubs. It was springtime, and the legend says that from the roots to the tips of the branches the grove was one mass of flowers, and from the midst of the shrubbery came the hum of bees and bird songs and the cries of peacocks.

The queen commanded her caravan to stop and rest, while she strolled for a while in this grove. She moved from thicket to thicket, from tree to tree, among the flowers; and then at the foot of a great satinwood tree she reached up her hand to touch a low branch which seemed to bend as if to greet her. Just as she grasped this branch, she felt the first pang of birth. She cried out to her women who speedily came, bringing with them silken canopies which they hung on the branches like a curtain around Maya. The queen had her baby then and there, standing up, with the blossoms falling upon her, and without even removing her hand from the branch of the satinwood tree.

It was a beautiful boy, not raw and wrinkled like ordinary babies, but the color of creamy gold; not squalling and snarling, but emitting sweetly modulated and charming sounds similar to the bird songs round about.

Yes, we are knee-deep in legend here! Some of the Buddhist texts say further that on this occasion a great lotus flower sprang up from the earth, bursting it in twain; that joyful Hindu gods made their appearance in the air, revealing themselves up to the waist, and a stream of hot-and-cold running water issued from the sky, in which the baby was bathed. Buddhists have argued about this. Some of them have maintained that a child so pure as this one did not need to be bathed, that in fact he was born clean and bright as a jewel.

Some stories are even more incredible. They tell us that directly after his birth, this child stood on its feet, examined the four quarters of the earth, and then, while gods held a white parasol and jeweled fans over his head, he took seven steps toward the north, roaring like a lion, and proclaiming to the world that he was the chieftain of all of it.

This tale sounds as if it had been made up to please people who cannot imagine greatness except in terms of worldly power. Such a man was King Suddhodana.

When Maya brought her child back to him at Kapila-vastu, he completely forgot that it was the custom of the Gautama family to give names that recalled the pleasing qualities of rice. Instead he gave his son a conqueror's name: Siddhartha, "The Victorious One."

Siddhartha Gautama was placed in a cradle cushioned in the finest white cotton, where he lay "like molten gold in a crucible." The Brahmins came to view him there and they stared in amazement. "Rejoice, sire," they told the king, "for one of the mighty ones is born. Fortune is yours, sire, good fortune is yours!"

They said that they could see plainly on Siddhartha's small person all of the thirty-two signs that mark a man of noble destiny. Most of these magical signs are such that loving eyes might see on the body of any newborn baby: his frame was straight, his hands and feet were soft and tender, his ankles were like rounded shells, his skin was delicately soft, his jaw was strong as a lion's; and so on.

But there were other signs visible to the Brahmins that were occult and peculiar. They said that on the soles of the baby's feet were the designs of little wheels; that the small hairs of his body, instead of growing downward like other people's, grew upward, "blue-black, like eye-paint, in little curling rings and curling to the right." Most particularly they noted a curious cluster of hairs, not black, but white, where his eyebrows grew together, like a hairy mole or a tiny silver chrysanthemum. His head, furthermore, had a knob on it which gave it the shape of a royal turban.

If you look closely at the statues of Buddha, you can

Some modern Buddhas, like this bronze statue erected in the
1950's in Central Taiwan, look as ancient as the hills.
It is 72 feet high, the tallest Buddha in the world.
*Courtesy The Chinese Information Service*

often find some of these special signs indicated on them.

Siddhartha's birth is said to have taken place on the full moon of May. It caused a brilliant light to spread over the earth, an infinite and splendid radiance which penetrated even to the murky dark regions below the world. The deaf heard; the lame walked; bad-tempered people thought sweet thoughts; and everywhere the multitudinous gods of India sprang into the sky to dance, sing, and wave their glittering scarves about them.

There was a holy man named Asita who lived as a hermit in a cave of the Himalayas, where he spent his life staring at the eternal snows, immersed in thoughts of God. When suddenly his meditations were interrupted by this great light and the sound of heavenly music, he dragged his fixed eyes from their sublime contemplation. With uncanny knowledge, he realized that a great event had taken place on the plains below. He got to his feet and began to travel in the direction of the light, down from the mountains and across the low-lying hills towards Kapilavastu. At the entrance to the king's palace, he rapped on the gates and told the gatekeepers to lead him to King Suddhodana.

No doubt Asita was dressed in rotting rags. Certainly he had forgotten to comb his matted hair. Probably for years he had not eaten more than would feed a rabbit, so that his bones almost rattled as he stalked past the fine frescoes, across the polished floors of the royal palace. But it is the way of India to revere her holy men and to forgive them their careless habits. No one thought of denying Asita his wish; in fact, King Suddhodana himself received him, bowing to the ground. He made

Asita sit down on a fine chair and commanded the prince to be brought.

Siddhartha was carried in and Asita gazed on him lying "like shining gold beaten out by a very skillful smith." At first he praised the child and made the father beam. But then, to the king's alarm, the holy man turned aside and wept.

"Why are you weeping," exclaimed the king, "shedding tears and heaving sighs? Do you see any danger threatening the prince?"

And Asita replied, "I do not weep for the prince, and no danger threatens him. Nay, I weep for myself. Great king, I am old, full of years and worn with age. This prince without doubt shall attain the highest and most perfect wisdom. And I shall not live to see it. Therefore I weep, O king!"

This is the traditional story of the birth of Gautama Buddha as described in age-old legends. They were not recorded in his lifetime, but passed by word of mouth for two centuries until in the time of King Asoka, the great ruler of the Maurya Empire, and a convert to Buddhism, Buddhist scholarship began. The surviving traditions came to be regarded as sacred text, and in time were written down. But whether spoken or written, they grew and changed. The parts people liked best to hear, the miracles and the tales of royal extravagance, became ever more elaborate, and many dry facts dropped out.

Modern scholars, historians, anthropologists, philologists, and archaeologists have looked closely into the

legends, comparing them one with the other, and they have examined other evidence in an effort to rescue the "historical Buddha." They agree that a man who came to be called the Buddha really lived, and they fix the date of his birth at about 563 B.C.

Kapilavastu was probably one of the many small city-states that peppered northern India in those early times. But within the next hundred and fifty years, they were caught in the giant net of the early Magadha and Maurya empires. In being unified, they were submerged, and eventually they disappeared, so that today no one knows which of the many mounds or piles of ruins scattered across this anciently settled region of India was once Kapilavastu.

A thousand years after the death of Buddha, a Chinese pilgrim, Fa Hien, was shown some ruins which he was told were the remains of King Suddhodana's palace. Three hundred years later, another Chinese pilgrim, Hiuen Tsiang, also saw some ruins, including the bedroom of Queen Maya and Prince Siddhartha's study. But we do not know that these traveling gentlemen were shown the same ruins; and their accounts only go to prove that tourist-guides in old India were just as eager to show people what they wanted to see as they are today.

More convincing is a pillar standing within the borders of Nepal with an inscription which says that it was erected by King Asoka and that it marks the site of the Lumbini Grove, the birthplace of Buddha. Of course the pillar does not prove that this spot is really the Lumbini Grove; it only proves that King Asoka thought it was. Still, Asoka was an intelligent man and a scholar in his own right, and furthermore, he lived just over two hundred years after the death of Buddha. The chances are strong that if nobody has moved his pillar in the centuries that passed until it was discovered only seventy years ago, it marks the veritable spot where Buddhists believe the founder of their religion was born.

Siddhartha was not necessarily the son of a ruler or the heir to a throne. Suddhodana may have been just a chieftain of the Sakya Clan, one of many such chieftains who bore the title of *raja*, king, just as many small land-owners in India bear this title at the present time. Nevertheless, it is likely that Siddhartha's father was a man of some standing among the Sakyas, perhaps a sort of paramount chieftain. Traditions have come down to us in which Buddha seems to tell us in his own words what his life was like, growing up as the adored son of a rich and influential father.

No trace of the Sakya Clan remains in India today, but it is interesting that there are people living in the region where the Sakya Clan is said to have flourished, who bear the family name of Gautama. They are Hindus, as of course Buddha was a Hindu, and they belong to the same caste, the Kshatriya, in which Siddhartha was born.

When all tangible evidence and all information to be gleaned from the birth-legends have been examined, we are left with few historic facts: only that a son was born once to a well-to-do Hindu family, and that it probably happened in the sixth century before Christ.

It was in many ways one of the most remarkable of centuries, a time when in various parts of the world old things were coming to an end and new ages dawning.

Twenty-four years before Buddha was born, Jerusalem was destroyed, and the last king of the line of David disappeared into a Babylonian prison. In Buddha's lifetime the Persian Empire was founded by Cyrus the Great; while Egypt, which for milennia had lorded it over the ancient world, fell under Persian rule.

Italy was dominated by the proud Tarquins, kings of Etruria; but the citizens of a rough little town called Rome threw off the Etruscan yoke and embarked upon an experiment with an unusual style of government: a republic.

The first of the wise Greeks, Solon the lawgiver, lived at the beginning of the sixth century, and Pythagoras the mathematician and philosopher lived at the end of it. The Golden Age of Greece began in Buddha's lifetime.

In China, an unsuccessful political philosopher, Confucius, vainly sought some king or duke who would give him a job in government. Not far away, the librarian of a decaying library, Lao-tzu, was writing all his wisdom in a book. When he had done, he mounted a water buffalo and rode off to the west, never to be heard from again. But the thoughts of these two sages, together with those of Gautama Buddha, would form the very warp and woof of the Chinese civilization.

The sixth century before Christ might well be called the Century of Wisdom; it was as if man, having found out how to feed, clothe, and shelter himself and otherwise manage the world around him, had now begun to look inward, into the spirit, to see what world lay there.

# 2

# Growing Up

*Now who is this? Is it Brahma or Siva? Or the God of Love? Or Krishna?*

MAHAVASTU

When Siddhartha Gautama was seven days old his mother died, but Buddhists do not mourn her. The old books say that as a mortal woman Maya would have been heartbroken to see her child grow up to be a homeless beggar. As it was, she went to live in the Heaven of Delight where she watched with pride the drama of her son's life unfolding.

Siddhartha was brought up by his aunt, Prajapati, who became Suddhodana's second wife, and she loved him as if he were her own. She provided him with thirty-two nurses, eight to carry him, eight to give him milk, eight to bathe him, and eight to play with him. Long afterward, Buddha was to describe his life in Kapilavastu: "I was tenderly cared for, monks, supremely so, infinitely so. At my father's home lotus-pools were made for me: one for blue lotus-flowers, another for white lotus-flowers, and another for red lotus-flowers, all blossoming for my sake.

"And monks, I used only the perfumes of Benares, and my clothes were made of Benares cloth. Day and night a white umbrella was held over me so that I might not be troubled by cold, heat, dust, chaff, or dew."

His father doted on him. King Suddhodana is remembered as industrious, conscientious and just, a ruler who "lived within the Law and obeyed the Law," and he had every intention of bringing up his son to be a competent man of affairs like himself. Indeed, the birth-predictions had implanted in his mind an even more dazzling ambition, for they had suggested that Siddhartha might become a Universal Monarch. This could be none other than the fabulous Chakravarti, whose coming was prophesied by the seers of old. From the veranda of his jeweled palace it was said that the benign and virtuous Chakravarti would fling forth a magic wheel which would roll farther than the mind can imagine until it embraced the globe, and wherever it appeared the races and nations of men would gladly place themselves under his rule.

And so, even when Siddhartha was so small that he had to be held astride his father's hip, he was made to sit in the judgment hall where he watched and listened while the Sakyas brought before the king an endless procession of worldly and selfish argument. In time, to his father's delight, Siddhartha learned the law of his land well enough to pronounce fair judgments of his own, and the onlookers smiled and clapped, and they said of him, "A seer! A seer!"

When Siddhartha was eight he was taken to the school of a renowned teacher who was astonished to find that his pupil could already read and write all the alphabets in India, as well as the strange ideographs of the Chinese and the Mongols.

Perhaps we catch a less fabulous glimpse of Siddhartha when we see him with his cousins, Devadatta and Ananda, practicing knightly skills such as horsemanship and archery, chariot-racing and wrestling, jousting and lance-throwing—strenuous sports which in time of war were used in dead earnest for the power and protection of the Sakya tribe. Several legends suggest that the prince took little pleasure in these games. In contest with the bow he would purposely miss his mark rather than inflict upon his opponent the pain of losing. He had no heart for wrestling, and he detested hunting. Eventually he gave up athletic sports, and often, while the boys played, he would wander off in the woods, kicking aimlessly at sticks and roots, and doubtless wondering, as thoughtful young people do, who he really was and who had put him on the earth and for what purpose.

One day while his comrades were hunting and Siddhartha sat alone in a grove, a splendid flight of swans streamed across the sky. His cousin Devadatta let fly an arrow which caught the lead swan on the wing, and it faltered and fell lamely to the ground close to Siddhartha. The prince approached the bird, which submitted to his gentle touch, and allowed him to pull out the arrow and staunch the wound with wild honey. Siddhartha was cradling the wounded swan in his arms when the boys

came scampering out of the woods, Devadatta breath-
lessly claiming his prize. "There's my swan!"

"It is not your swan," said Siddhartha.

"It is! I killed it and it's mine!"

"You did not kill the swan," replied Siddhartha bitterly,
"but only the power of its swift flight."

The argument was taken to Suddhodana who ordered
the matter put before his Brahmins. They decided for
Siddhartha. "Devadatta strove to take away the bird's
life," they said. "Siddhartha gave back its life. He who
gives life is more worthy to own the creature than he
who takes life away. Even the gods cannot give back life
when it is lost."

This was a wise judgment, but it earned trouble for
Siddhartha. His cousin Devadatta was eaten by resentment and in the future he was to become Gautama's
enemy. But Siddhartha never lost the love of his cousin
Ananda who became his closest friend; and if these tales
of Gautama's youth have any truth in them, it was
perhaps Ananda who first told them when he was old
and living on memories of his Teacher.

King Suddhodana was watching with increasing un-
easiness his son's gentle habits which were altogether un-
suitable to a boy of his caste. The Kshatriya was the
second highest of the Hindu castes, the one to which
princes, rulers, and warriors belonged. The highest caste
was that of the Brahmins (who invented the caste system): they were the priests, wise men, and teachers.
Below Siddhartha on the scale were the Vaisyas, the
merchants and tradesmen; and next the Sudras, the

peasants. At the very lowest level were the outcastes whom in our own day we have heard called "Untouchables." They performed the very poorest work, that of sweeping the streets and clearing away refuse.

Chakravarti, the Universal Monarch, was, of course, destined to be born a Kshatriya. But Prince Siddhartha was behaving more like a Brahmin, disinterested in the intricate business of ruling a country, caring nothing for the supremacy of the Sakyas over other tribes, bored even with the fun of being a prince, the splendor and processional, the feats on horseback, the languishing glances of the girls. Suddhodana, seeing his indifference, was troubled and perplexed.

One spring day when Siddhartha was sixteen years old, he went to the fields to watch the festival of the spring plowing when the ground was broken and made level to receive new seed. The king himself handled the first plow, which was made of gold, and he was followed by a thousand nobles with silver plows. Then came the ordinary farmers with their wooden ones, but on this day their rough implements were gaily decorated with ribbons and flowers; the horns of the oxen gleamed with bright paint and their sides had been polished until they glowed like satin. For all the tribe it was a day of rejoicing, full of the promise of new life.

Siddhartha's companions dispersed to follow the girls. The prince seated himself under the shade of a rose apple tree. Somehow the prevailing merriment failed to touch him. He found his mind dwelling not on the promise of new life, but on the pathos of life in general. The farmers were dressed in their best clothes, but the sweat streamed down their corded legs as usual; the oxen wore garlands of flowers, but they strained and grunted as they always did. The ground broke into rich black lumps, but the meadow birds streaked into the sky lamenting their ruined nests, and the rabbits fled their burrows. Some raucous person held up the body of a snake slashed in two. Siddhartha might have wondered whether it was worth while pitying moles, ants, and grasshoppers, but nevertheless he pitied them, for if one decides to place value on life, which life can one leave out?

The boy's thoughts slid away from these tragedies, plunged into some quiet well of the mind below consciousness where the nature of man becomes immersed with the nature of things. And then, so the legend says, Nature herself took notice of this young communicant, and as the afternoon passed and the turning shadows shifted, the shadow of the rose apple tree did not desert Siddhartha, but stood still and sheltered him.

This episode is known as the First Trance; it was Gautama Buddha's youthful step from the world of action to the world of the spirit.

King Suddhodana, when he heard of it, exhausted as he was by his unaccustomed labors, was not pleased. He did not dream that the memory of it would be treasured for thousands of years. For him it was only a reminder that his son's mind was caught in the subtle snare of reflection, and that somehow or other it must be wooed away. He called his privy councilors together and asked them what was to be done about Siddhartha.

The privy councilors were old and wily, and they had brought up sons of their own. They well knew the reason for the prince's melancholia: he was of marriageable age, and he must get married.

The king was elated by this sudden solution to his worries, and he lost no time in sending letters to the Sakya nobles: "My son is grown. Let all send the young maidens, their daughters, to the palace."

Accordingly, the noble Sakyas arrayed their daughters in the precious stuffs of their dowries and sent them to the palace where Siddhartha received them one by one. The king had caused a large number of jeweled ornaments of gold, silver, and lapis lazuli to be fashioned especially for this occasion, with some especially fine ones for Siddhartha to give to the girls he most admired, and these were placed on a tray beside his hand. As each young woman approached the prince and stood before him, head bent, hands folded, while her name was pronounced to him, he picked up a jewel and presented it to her. This scene was witnessed from the background by the privy councilors, who watched him sharply to detect any glance or lingering touch of the hand that might indicate that his interest had been captured; but their attentiveness was all in vain. Siddhartha was courteous to every girl, but he handed out his jewels indiscriminately, hardly glancing at the maidens, who, sensing his indifference, were embarrassed and scurried off with a soft jingle of ankle bells.

At length all jewels and girls had been used up, and

the prince rose to depart. At that moment there entered the hall a late-comer, Yasodhara, daughter of a Sakya noble. Now the prince was embarrassed, for he had no jewels left, and Yasodhara, grasping the situation, decided to have some fun with it. She approached Siddhartha, eyeing the empty tray, and standing before him gazed mockingly into his eyes: "Prince, what have I done to you that you despise me?"

"I despise you not," protested Siddhartha, "but you have come last of all." Then he astonished her by taking from his neck a magnificent necklace and clasping it around her waist.

"I am not worthy of it," she whispered.

"Take all of them," replied Siddhartha, and began to divest himself of a fortune in ornaments.

They fell in love. Years later, Gautama was to explain to his disciples the reason for their swift delight in each other: that Yasodhara had been his wife in countless lifetimes past; that once they had been tigers together roaming in the sun-streaked jungle; and once Yasodhara had been a maiden selling lotus-flowers to a conceited young divinity student named Megha.

Her father, however, knew nothing of this. He, and many other Sakya nobles, were resentful of the high-handed manner in which this perfectly useless prince had taken his choice of their daughters. For years none of them had seen Siddhartha raise a bow; no longer did he sit at his father's side in the judgment hall; his teacher had long since given up teaching him, and for all they knew he had given up in despair.

Now King Suddhodana sat silent and dejected in his palace.

"O king, why are you so sad at heart?" asked Siddhartha.

"Young man, say no more!" snapped Suddhodana.

"It is better we should speak," insisted the prince, and when he had three times insisted, his father told him the humiliating truth: that Yasodhara's father had refused to give her hand in marriage unless Siddhartha could win her in athletic and intellectual contests against all other suitors. "Can you prove yourself, my son?" asked Suddhodana anxiously. And Siddhartha said, "Let all those exercised in skills assemble together, that I may show it."

Tales of how young men have contested for the hand of a fair maiden by feats of strength and daring are familiar the world over; they are among the most ancient stories ever told. Very likely those that tell how Siddhartha competed against his cousins and other young men for Yasodhara's hand were old before any of them were born.

In archery competition all the contestants placed their drums at immense distances, but Siddhartha placed his drum so far away that it seemed to be the size of a cowrie shell; and yet his arrow pierced all the drums and his own as well. In a feat of strength, Devadatta killed an elephant with one blow. Another young noble, Sunderananda, after reproving Devadatta for his cruelty, twirled the elephant by its tail and flung it outside the city gates of Kapilavastu. Siddhartha, after reproving Sunderananda for untidiness, lightly lifted his toe and kicked the elephant to the other side of a mountain.

In swordsmanship, Devadatta clove the trunk of a tree six fingers thick, and the sword of an opponent, Arjuna, cut one of nine fingers. Siddhartha flashed through two such trees together and the trees still stood upright, so that his adversaries jumped for joy, thinking that his blade had turned; but the watchful angels gently blew on the trees and they toppled to the ground.

Siddhartha bent a bow that no one had bent since his grandfather's time, and its string made a sound of thunder for miles around. He tamed a savage horse that no one else could tame by turning its face to the sun so that it would not be frightened by its own shadow. The next time this story was told, it was told of Alexander the Great.

The contests continued: quick-walking, swimming, use of elephant goad and lasso; calligraphy, medicine, astronomy, arithmetic; the occult sciences; answering riddles; explaining dreams; charades; telling jokes; imitating birds.

Siddhartha won them all and regained the good opinion of his clansmen. Yasodhara became his bride.

The figure of Yasodhara is as shadowy in the legends as the hushed sound of her name; and yet she has had more influence on the lives of more women than any other person in history or legend.

For it seems that Yasodhara, unlike other Hindu ladies of her time, objected to holding her veil across her face.

She did not make this decent gesture in the presence of her stepmother-in-law, Prajapati, nor in that of the king, nor before respected Brahmins, nor before anyone. Criticism was inevitable, and people said of her, "This young woman is surely not modest."

When Yasodhara became aware of this talk, she came before the assembled court and gave them a piece of her mind. "Those whose thoughts have no cover," she said, "who have no shame or decorum or any virtue and who gossip, may cover themselves with a thousand garments, yet do they walk the earth naked. But those who veil their minds, control their senses, and have no thought for any other except their husband, why should they veil their faces?"

Suddhodana was delighted with his daughter-in-law's proud statement and he gave her two white costumes covered with jewels, which she thoroughly deserved, for she had spared Buddhist women from having to wear veils forever after.

# 3

# The Great Renunciation

*They who have lost their foothold fall. But they can, if they will, arise again and yet again.*

THERAGATA

In years to come, Buddha would describe the opulence of his married life: "I had three palaces, one for the cold season, one for the hot, and one for the season of rains. Through the four rainy months, in the palace for the rainy season, entertained by female minstrels, I did not come down from the palace."

King Suddhodana did not hesitate to shower extravagant gifts upon the newlyweds; he was overjoyed to have found a snare to keep his son from the dangerous habit of thinking. One of the palaces he presented to the young couple was built in marble fretted and pinnacled like a wedding cake; and another was of wood carved until it looked like a palace made of lace; and another was of brick, stuccoed, painted, and frescoed. All were lively with musicians, storytellers, dancing girls, and jugglers who entertained the prince as he sat in jeweled bowers perfumed with cinnamon and tuberose. Around the palaces, Suddhodana spread a pleasure park which extended far and wide under the blinding Himalayas; and it was set with glorious groves of mangrove and willow, ornamental gardens, playing courts, pools, and fountains from which fish like jewels leapt, and exotic birds were everywhere to be seen. When Siddhartha went walking—if we are to believe the wondrous sculptures on the great temple at Borobudur in Java—he was followed by bevies of handmaidens bearing trays of sherbets, cakes, fruits, musical instruments, bowls of flowers, fly-whisks, fans, and similar conveniences. His companions were richly dressed young nobles who carried flowers about with them to show that they never did any work.

Yasodhara is there too, by her husband's side, in her tall headdress.

Compassion, Suddhodana knew, was his son's besetting sin. It was this emotion that stung his sensitive mind and provoked him to inward wondering. The Brahmins had foretold that Gautama's obsession with man's pain might cause him to leave his home and go forth into the world as a beggar. Therefore Suddhodana commanded that no word or hint of sorrow, sickness, or death, or any betrayal of the pathetic impermanence of material things should ever be spoken anywhere near the prince.

No bad news was ever to be told him; no sign of sorrow was to mar the countenance of anyone about him. Should any dancer feel weary and her feet fail in nimbleness, she was to be whisked out of his sight. The appearance of a silver hair on anyone's head or beard meant swift banishment from the prince's household. Even the wicks in the oil lamps were not allowed to grow dim, the oils being constantly replenished; and cohorts of gardeners swarmed over the grounds at dawn, plucking every drooping rose, sweeping up dead leaves.

Siddhartha's world was as neat and perfect as a Persian painting; and lest he should catch a glimpse of any other kind of world, the king enclosed the pleasure park with a huge wall and set hundreds of guards upon it, and he had stout gates made, so heavy that it took five hundred Sakyas to open them, and they were fashioned so that the noise of their opening squealed throughout Kapila-vastu.

In love with his wife, enthralled by a never-ending succession of delights, Siddhartha recovered from his youthful melancholia, and the legend asks us to believe that as the years passed he gradually forgot that mankind bore such burdens as sickness, old age, or death; and he lived a willing prisoner in his oriental Eden.

One would think that King Suddhodana spent these years sleeping peacefully at night, but he did not; he was plagued by bad dreams. One night he saw in a dream his son, dressed as a monk in a rough robe, leaving his home; and this made him sit up straight in bed. "Is my son in the palace?" he asked, and the servant replied, "He is, O king." But the king was in a fright, and he consulted a soothsayer who told him that while his efforts had been thorough, they were not thorough enough. He must build another pleasure park even more delightful than the present one, which, if the prince set eyes on it but once, he would never wish to leave.

King Suddhodana leapt to the task. He dispatched an army of landscape gardeners to lay out a park of supreme loveliness with a thousand vistas, and pools set like gems in the greensward. It was called the Garden of Happiness, and the prince was enchanted to hear about it. He promised to go on a tour of inspection.

There was a difficulty. The new park was situated some little distance from Kapilavastu, and in order to visit it, the prince would have to pass out of his estates and travel through the public streets. King Suddhodana gave orders that on the great day every inch of the town was to be swept, cleaned, and polished to unexampled brightness, and potted plants set in front of ugly spots. The houses were to be newly painted and hung with silks and flowers, the people were to wear their best clothes, and—most particularly—every aged or deformed or invalid person, every work-gnarled laborer, everyone who was not young, handsome, and bounding with life, was to be hidden from sight.

Siddhartha set out in his state chariot, accompanied by his charioteer, Channa. The gates of his domain screamed at his going. He passed through the pretty streets of Kapilavastu, smiling and greeting his handsome, prosperous subjects who were strewing his path with flowers and scents, and he left the city by the East Gate, having seen nothing to awaken his mind from its oblivion. But the gods were awake, and they had prepared an adventure for Siddhartha.

No sooner had the prince left the city than he saw on the path before him a dreadful sight; it was an old man, aged, worn-out, with swollen veins on his body and broken, chattering teeth. He was wrinkled and gray-haired, bent at the angle of a gabled roof, leaning on a stick and trembling in all his limbs, and from his throat came inarticulate sounds.

"Who is that man?" cried Siddhartha to Channa. "Why is his hair not like that of other men?"

And the charioteer, inspired by the gods, heard himself telling the prince the forbidden truth. "He is what is called an aged man, my lord."

"But why is he called aged?"

"Because he has not much longer to live," replied Channa.

"But then, good charioteer, am I too subject to old age?"

"You are, my lord, and so are we all."

Siddhartha then gave up all thought of visiting the Garden of Happiness, and returned to the palace where he retired to his apartments to ponder what he had learned. "Shame," he thought, "upon this thing called birth, since to one born, old age shows itself like that."

Channa meanwhile was confessing what had happened to King Suddhodana, who was dismayed. He gave orders for magnificent gifts to be sent to the prince, imaginative games, new dancing girls, and magicians who knew exotic tricks.

Siddhartha allowed himself to be wooed from his worries and again fell into his easy habits. In time he decided to set forth again for the pleasure park. As before, he passed through the immaculate streets of the town, and left it this time by the South Gate. No sooner had he gained the open countryside than he saw, lying beside the road, a wretched creature, ill of fever, with bloodshot eyes, groaning and breathing in gasps; and he was abandoned there without shelter from the sun or anyone to help him, for he was altogether loathsome in his filth.

"That man, Channa," exclaimed the prince, "what is the matter with his eyes? Why is he making noises like that?"

"He is ill, my lord," replied Channa.

"And what is meant by ill?"

"It means, my lord, that his body is diseased and in pain."

"But am I too subject to fall ill?"

"You are, and so are we all."

Now Siddhartha told Channa to turn back, and again he shut himself in his rooms "trembling like the moon on rippled water," and thinking, "Shame upon this thing called birth, since to one born, disease shows itself like that!" And again his father provided frolics to distract him.

A third time Siddhartha set out for the Garden of Happiness, by still another gate, but he did not escape his fated lesson. This time his eyes fell upon a group of people in weird procession. There was the form of a dead man laid out on a bier under a linen sheet surrounded by a troop of his relations, all weeping, lamenting, and wailing, with streaming hair and ashes on their heads.

"What is the matter with them, why do they smear dirt on their heads, and what is that thing they are carrying?" asked the prince.

"It is someone who has ended his days, and they are mourning him," replied Channa.

"Drive close to him," commanded the prince, and when Channa did so, Siddhartha looked upon the corpse. "What does it mean, Channa, to end one's days?" he whispered.

"It means, my lord, that neither mother nor father nor wife nor kinsmen will ever see him again, for he is dead."

"Shall I too be dead? Will not the king nor my aunt Prajapati, nor my wife or friends, see me again, nor shall I see them?"

"Yes, my lord, we are all subject to death."

"And what after death?"

Channa told him the belief of every Hindu: one is reborn to live through similar tragedies all over again.

"Then turn back, Channa," said Siddhartha. And he went to his rooms in desolation, thinking, "Shame on this thing called birth, since to one born, death shows itself like that."

Now when Suddhodana heard what had happened, he rushed into the prince's palace bellowing commands. "Let music never cease!" he cried. "Let all kinds of play and amusement be provided simultaneously. Let the women use all their powers of attraction!" Again he sent diversions to his son, and again Siddhartha's spirit was dimmed by pleasure; and once more he set out for the Garden of Happiness, leaving the city through still another gate.

But the gods had not done with him. This time, one of them appeared to him in the form of a shaven-headed man in a rough robe. He stood by the side of the road, quiet, serene of countenance, and discreet. His eyes did not raise to admire the prince's splendor—indeed they did not seem to see anything more than a few paces in front of him. He simply stood there with his begging bowl, and peace was with him.

"Who is that?" murmured the prince.

"It is a monk, my lord, one who has gone forth."

"What do you mean by 'gone forth'?"

"He has gone forth from his home to lead a simple, religious life, to find peace of mind through good actions, harmlessness, and kindness to all creatures."

"Drive me home," said the prince.

Siddhartha returned to his apartments violently agitated, and now no pleasure that his father put before him could tempt him from his thoughts. He had seen the truth of mortal life: old age, sickness, death; and he had seen neglect and poverty, suffering and grief; yet he had glimpsed also a man who seemed to have found a way of salvation.

He perceived that for years he had allowed himself to be deceived, and that all the pomp with which his father had surrounded him was but a cloak to hide the real nature of things. For no one was happy. Love was not happiness. His father loved him, but Siddhartha realized with a shock that he had brought nothing but anxiety to his father.

He wandered in the night around his halls, saw his dancing girls and handmaidens asleep like wilted flowers on the floor, and suddenly their loveliness was rent away from them. Some had their dresses in disorder and their hair disheveled, some sprawled in clumsy attitudes with their mouths open, some sweated, coughed, sniffled, and muttered in their sleep.

He looked upon his dear Yasodhara, but perhaps she was the most deceptive of all, for he knew now that her shining person was but the dwelling place of decay and death, and that nothing in creation could ever endure. "I am living in a graveyard!" he said to himself.

The solution was born in his mind: he must renounce his possessions, leave his home, go forth into the world penniless, and seek the divine secret he had sensed in the presence of the monk.

Then he would find a way of teaching it to others.

It would have been rank ingratitude to his father to go without informing him of his decision. And so, in the soundless night, he went to the apartments of the king. Suddhodana awoke from his sleep to see his son standing by his bed. Siddhartha said, "Hinder me no more, and be not sorrowful; for the hour of my departure is come."

The king wept. He exhorted his son to remain in his palace. "I will stay," said Siddhartha, "if you will grant me four favors."

"Anything!" cried the king.

"Grant me," said Siddhartha, "that old age shall never take possession of me, that illness never ravage me, and that I shall never die; and that you and Yasodhara and all others I love shall remain the same always."

"These things I cannot grant you," said Suddhodana sorrowfully.

Siddhartha told him that he would leave before the full moon.

The king was beside himself. He placed a cordon of five hundred men around the steps of the prince's palace; and the guard at the walls and at the gateway was strengthened by thousands of Sakyas.

Siddhartha's foster mother, Prajapati, commanded his handmaidens, "Light up bright lamps, never let them fail, place all sorts of reflecting jewels upon the stands, hang necklaces about, and illuminate the whole dwelling. Cause music to sound day and night. Arm yourselves with quivers, swords, bows, arrows, spears, javelins, lances. And watch him narrowly."

Thus Siddhartha found his every movement watched; he was encircled in a "cage of gold." But there was a guard upon him more compelling than any that his father could command, and this was his love for his wife.

Siddhartha and Yasodhara were both twenty-nine years old. They had been married for more than ten years, and had longed for a child. Now by the time of the full moon, Yasodhara was going to give birth, and notwithstanding his resolve, the prince could not bear the thought of leaving her, of never seeing the face of his child. As the days passed and Yasodhara's time approached, his will weakened.

On the day of the full moon, he was strolling with some companions by the riverside at the far reaches of his estate when word was brought to him that Yasodhara had borne him a son. "Here is another fetter that I must cut!" he groaned, "and so let Rahula—fetter—be his name."

It was late when he came with his company back to the palace and fear gripped his heart, because he knew

that should he once set eyes upon his son he would never summon the strength to keep his resolve.

Then, just as he passed a wing of the palace, he heard from the terrace the voice of a young girl singing him a song of welcome and congratulation. She leaned over the balcony and sang:

> *Happy indeed is the mother,*
> *Happy indeed is the father,*
> *Happy indeed is the wife*
> *Who has such a husband.*

Now in the language Siddhartha spoke, the word for "happy" is the same as that for "free." The word is familiar, even to us, in its Sanskrit form, *nirvana.* The young girl's song had reminded Siddhartha of the deceptiveness of one's emotions. His love for his son, Rahula, was a fetter, and ought not to be confused with happiness, which was synonymous with freedom, deliverance, salvation.

He took from his neck a string of pearls of great price and had them carried to the singing girl who received them in astonishment, thinking that the prince had fallen in love with her; but he had forgotten her entirely. He went to his apartments deep in thought, and he did not visit his wife and son.

He called Channa, and told him to have his horse Kantala ready and waiting that very night. When all the palace was silent with sleep, he arose from his couch and left his rooms—and if there were handmaidens standing about with raised javelins narrowly watching him, the

gods blinded their bright eyes. Yet, as Siddhartha passed
his wife's door, he found that he could not go by it
without looking upon his son; and in spite of the risk he
ran of becoming once again love's prisoner, he opened
the door and silently entered.

A lamp of scented oil was burning, and on the bed
strewn with jessamine and other flowers, the mother of
Rahula lay asleep. Siddhartha stood with his feet on the
threshold and strained to see the child; but he could not.
Yasodhara's hand was resting on her son's head. "If I
move aside her hand," he thought, "she will wake and
prevent my going. I must not see my son." Then he
turned and left his home, his wealth, his power, his wife
and child.

Channa waited for him with Kantala, and Siddhartha
mounted with Channa behind. The watchful gods muffled
the sound of the horse's foosteps, and when they arrived
at the gate which is called the Gate of Salvation, the
hundreds of Sakyas who stood guard there fell into a
deep sleep. The huge bars dropped away, and the scream-
ing gates seemed to have been miraculously oiled, for
they swung open silently and Siddhartha passed outside.

But he was by no means free: a dreadful apparition
stood across his path. It was Mara, the Evil One, the
Tempter, the lord of luxury, passions, and lusts, the
purveyor of all impermanent delights. For years he had
been ruling the life of the prince, using Suddhodana as
his tool, and now he saw his vassal escaping. In essence
Mara was a crude fellow, but he spoke politely on this
occasion: "Sir, depart not. On the seventh day from now

the jewel-wheel of empire will appear, and thou shalt rule over the four great islands and the two hundred small islands that surround them."

It was the tempting image of Chakravarti again. But if Siddhartha had not been held back by Rahula, Chakravarti could not move him. He ignored Mara and pressed swiftly on. Furious, the Evil One let himself relax into his usual scowl, and he uttered a vicious threat: "Very well, go your way, but remember this: henceforth, whenever thou hast a thought of lust or malice or cruelty, I shall know it."

And seeking mastery over the mind of Siddhartha, Mara slunk after him "on the watch for any failing, cleaving to him like a shadow which follows the object from which it falls."

This tradition of the Great Renunciation has been told in poetry and prose, in painting and in sculpture, for centuries, and it has been taught to their children by people who no doubt believed every word of it. It seems obvious that the "Four Signs," the apparitions of old age, sickness, death, and salvation were inventions devised by the legend-makers to teach, to inspire, and to hold people spellbound.

But where is the "historical Buddha"?

In later years after Gautama became a great teacher, his recollections of his luxurious youth became a subject of discourse between himself and his monks. Perhaps some truth survives for us in them. In one discourse he mentioned that when he was a boy he had fallen into a trance. The legend-makers built upon this remark until it became the popular tradition of the rose apple tree with its motionless shadow.

One thing seems certain: a Renunciation must have taken place. At some time in the ancient world an extremely intelligent young Kshatriya with a natural disposition to thoughtfulness must have decided to renounce the position he had been born to fill and leave home to become a begging monk. The oldest canonical account of the event has Buddha relating it quite simply:

"I thought, oppressive is life in a house, a place of dust. Not easy is it for him who dwells in a house to practice a completely full, pure, and perfect religious life. What if I remove my hair and beard and go forth from a house to a houseless life?

"While yet a boy, a black-haired lad in the prime of youth, in the first stage of my life, while my unwilling mother and father wept with tear-stained faces, I cut off my hair and beard and went forth from a house to a houseless life."

No hint is given here of the romantic legend just told or that Siddhartha was married and the father of a son or owned a horse named Kantala. But the fact that this legend is the oldest does not necessarily mean that it is truer than the romantic story, which may have been based upon still older traditions that were never recorded, or of which the records are lost.

The enduring tradition is that, motivated by compassion, Siddhartha Gautama broke the fetters of a worldly life; and that he left home determined to think through the enigma of human suffering so that he might point a way out of it.

# 4

# The Noble Quest

*I am naught of anyone anywhere, nor is there anywhere aught of mine.*

ANGUTTARA-NIKAYA

Mounted on his white steed, Siddhartha streamed silently under the moon away from Kapilavastu. When he was still within sight of the city he started to turn Kantala in order to look once more upon his home; but the gods, to spare him the ordeal, caused the earth to give a little spin beneath his feet, and he did not pause but pressed onward. He left the territory of the Sakyas behind him, crossed the kingdom of the Koliyas and that of the Mallas. He traveled forty-five miles between midnight and dawn and did not stop until he reached the bank of the river Anoma, which is thought to be a branch of the modern river Rapti.

He crossed the river on Kantala, but then dismounted. With a sweep of his sword he cut off his long hair and beard, the symbols of his high caste, and tossed them to the sky. Then he handed his sword and jewelry to Channa and told him to take them with the horse back to

Kapilavastu. Weeping, the charioteer took leave of his master and departed. A thousand years later there were shrines marking the place where Channa turned back.

Siddhartha proceeded toward the sunrise. Presently he saw a man in the forest wearing the buff leather robes of a huntsman. It occurred to him that his own fine garments were hardly suitable as a costume for a wandering beggar, and so he stopped the man and induced him—without much difficulty—to make an exchange. Now he was no longer Prince Siddhartha, but Gautama, the yellow-clad monk. A thoughtful god appeared and gave him a begging bowl.

He was making for Rajagriha, the capital of Magadha, a state somewhat more powerful than the petty principalities of the region, whose ruler at that time was King Bimbasara. As he went his way he caught up with a herdsman who was urging a flock of sheep in the same direction. Gautama noticed a curious little drama going on in the flock: a certain ewe had two lambs, one of which was wounded in the leg, and the poor ewe was having a hard time. She jostled back and forth between the healthy lamb who kept bounding forward and the lame one lagging behind, and she bleated unceasingly, belabored always by the hard stick of the herdsman.

"I will watch over this little one for you, wherever you are going," said Gautama, and he picked up the lame lamb and slung it across his neck. He paced along, near the ewe.

It occurred to him to ask the herdsman where he was going. The man replied that he was taking the sheep to the court of King Bimbasara where they would all be killed as a sacrifice to the gods.

"Then I'll go too," said Gautama, and he followed the flock into the city.

In the great Hall of Sacrifice the king stood with his Brahmins beside the sacrificial stone which streamed with the blood of victims; the king's sins were being transferred by magical means to the animals which then died for them, none too willingly.

Gautama entered with the lamb on his shoulders. Roughly clothed though he was, his princely manner had not deserted him; his gestures and manner were impressively royal, and when he asked leave to speak, the crowd listened. He spoke to them with tenderness of the miracle of life which none can give, though it may so easily be taken away; he told the king that if he would sacrifice to the gods his sinful desires instead of helpless lambs, it would make a better man of him.

The Brahmins looked ashamed, and the king gave orders that the sacrifice should cease.

This tale in which Gautama so easily dissuaded the priests from their religious duties is not altogether unbelievable. At the time Gautama lived, these political Brahmins with their vulgar rituals were under fire from all directions. Blood sacrifice was being denounced by the most advanced Brahmin thinkers. At that very hour, in the same region, lived Mahavira, founder and teacher of the Jain Sect, whose followers to this day sweep the ground before them as they walk lest they should step on an ant. Gautama's voice was the voice of his times. No doubt the king and the Brahmins too were disgusted by the horrid ritual, and were thankful for an excuse to be done with it.

Gautama left the Hall of Sacrifice and mingled with the crowd on the streets. He had not eaten throughout the day, and now he began to beg his food from door to door. Everywhere he went the householders felt the impact of his presence, and silently they placed in his bowl the leavings from their humble tables.

He went outside the city gates and sat down under a tree to eat. But he found that he could not. Hungry as he was, he was revolted by the wretched mess—such crude food as he had never seen before—and he could not get it as far as his mouth. He set his bowl aside and reflected, "I have gone forth from my home for a noble purpose, but it seems I am too weak to overcome the first obstacle. This food is detestable, but it will help me toward my goal, and I must therefore eat it."

After a while he found courage to pick up his bowl and eat.

The city of Rajagriha—which we know today as Rajgir—was situated in the eastern valley of the Ganges River, surrounded on the south by a range of hills which is the most northerly spur of the Vindhya Mountains. These hills were riddled with caves, ideal dwellings for hermits and ascetics, people who like Gautama had left their homes to live as holy men. The Chinese traveler, Hiuen Tsiang, described the place as it looked in the seventh century A.D.: "Tall peaks abruptly scarped, valleys and caves without end; swift torrents racing down the hills, and enormous forests in the valley. Tangles of bush and creeper shade the caverns. Above, shining through the mists and touching heaven itself, are three bold peaks."

For so many centuries did this wild region serve as a dwelling for ascetics that today we know the kingdom of Magadha by the name Bihar, from the old word *vihara,* meaning monastery.

Gautama now came to the mountains in search of a *guru,* a spiritual teacher. And it is at this stage of his life that a transformation takes place in the recorded story of his life. Up to this point the legend-makers, perhaps knowing little of his early life, have been entertaining us with a figure of fancy, and they have taken pains to keep our eyes round with wonder; they have bestowed upon him a miraculous birth and padded out his youth with supernatural events. But now, as Gautama climbs the Vindhya Mountains, the spangled veil lifts. The marvels do not cease by any means, but they are no longer the main fabric of the tale, which is that of a real man doing what other people did, walking on ground you may walk on yourself, and talking to people historians know. From this time on, the "historical Buddha" stands out from the legend with fair clarity.

A renowned teacher named Alara Kalama lived in these caverned hills and it was this man whom Gautama first sought out, and he said, "Brother Kalama, I would like to lead the religious life under your doctrine and discipline."

"Then remain," replied Alara Kalama, "because my

teaching is such that any intelligent man can learn it and profit by it."

Thereupon, Gautama sat down with the *guru's* other pupils and in no time at all learned how to recite the doctrine; and with the others he repeated over and over again with faith, "I know! I see!" But Gautama saw a thing that some of his fellow pupils did not: that it was not by faith alone that Alara had attained his wisdom, but by the hard work of thinking and understanding. "Alara has energy, mindfulness, concentration," he thought. "I too have them, and I am determined to understand his doctrine."

Alara was surprised and considerably impressed when in a short while his new pupil was able not only to repeat by heart, but to understand his abstruse doctrine as well as he did himself. "It is my gain," he said, "to have such a student."

Gautama, however, was not satisfied. "Where does it all lead?" he asked his teacher, and Alara replied, "It leads to the realm of Non-Existence."

There is, of course, such a thing as the realm of Non-Existence. It is a state of mind achieved by methodical practice of the trance. In later years Gautama was to introduce Alara's teaching into his own philosophical system. But for the present it did not seem to him to have been worth leaving his home and family to find the realm of Non-Existence.

He took his leave of Alara and next sought instruction from another famous teacher named Udraka. Again, Udraka's teaching, though Gautama grasped it, left him with the same feeling of futility as had Alara's. "Where does it lead?" he wanted to know, and Udraka told him that it led to a "state of Neither Perception nor Non-Perception."

Such a state of mind, teetering on the brink of transcendent knowledge, is perhaps a high attainment for a mystic, but it did not seem to contain a cure for human suffering. Gautama therefore took leave of Udraka. The *guru* was sorry to lose such a gifted pupil, and perhaps sorrier still to lose five of his disciples who, perceiving that Gautama was an unusual person, chose to follow him. "One day," said these five disciples to each other, "the ascetic Gautama will have his own Doctrine, and he will share it with us."

Perhaps in those early days of his quest, before he had learned to know his own nature, Gautama might have blamed himself for finding fault with the ideas of these esteemed mystics. Anyone who tries to do something new in this world must suffer self-doubt and a sense of separation from his fellow man. In fact, Gautama was in instinctive rebellion against a grave fault that was marring the religious life of his day. On the one hand there was the "popular religion" with its ritual worship of gods, much of it empty and some of it barbaric. On the other hand, there was "the philosophy" whose lively spirit of speculation was leading Hindu thinkers into sublime realms of metaphysics where the popular religion could not follow.

Thus the best thought of the time was taking flight away from the people. Moral life suffered, and intellectual life grew vague and vain when it moved too far from its base, the common earth.

Looking with hindsight at the great Teacher as he embarked upon his Noble Quest, we can discern in the legends how this state of affairs must have troubled him. Siddhartha Gautama was one of the most practical men who ever lived. His every word, as it has come down to us, breathes forth the concrete thinker. His arguments, parables, and images, though they are subtle, are homely and fashioned of the stuff of life. It was not merely to immerse himself in a fog of abstractions that he was making these excursions into the world of the spirit. He wanted to find out why men suffer, and how they could be delivered from suffering. He was after truths that could be used in the world of action.

Later, in recalling these holy men of the hills, Gautama remarked, "There are many ascetics who conceive night to be just the same as day, and day just the same as night. I call this being in love with illusion. As far as I am concerned, when night is here it is night; and when day is here it is day."

He was a rare genius: a great mystic who was also a practical man.

Today there are six philosophical systems in orthodox Hinduism. In Gautama's day they were not yet developed, but they were in the process of being developed, and he saw it happening. He saw the yogis practicing their queerly harmonious positions, breathing in and out with noises like the sound of rhythmic drums. And he saw fakirs,

people who believe that by undergoing extremities of
self-torture, they can crush the passions of the body and
thus achieve complete control of their minds. Some of
them sat in the middle of a close circle of fire; some
stared unceasingly at the sun; some held an arm in the
air for years until it withered; or lived on cow dung; or
sat on spikes.

Gautama and his companions listened to what these
people had to say of their methods, and afterward looked
around for a suitable place where they could try them
out. "Striving after the good and searching for the supreme
state of peace," he said, "I went to Uruvela, the army
town. There I saw a delightful spot with a pleasant grove,
a river flowing delightfully with clear water and a good
forest, and round about a place for seeking alms. . . . Then
I thought, this surely is a fit place for one who strives.
And I sat down there."

Perhaps he told his five companions the simile with
which he explained the point of such strivings: he said
that if one tries to strike fire by rubbing on wet green
wood, one cannot get fire. Nor can one hope to achieve
knowledge and enlightenment if the passions are not
calmed. But if one rubs on dry wood, fire is kindled.

To make themselves as dry of passion as that piece of
dry wood and so to kindle in themselves the fire of
supreme knowledge was the object of these six young
men. To this end they imposed upon themselves severe
penances. Years later Gautama described his sufferings
in the jungles of Uruvela: "I thought, suppose I set my
teeth, press my tongue to my palate and restrain, crush,

burn out my mind with my mind? I did so, and sweat poured from my armpits. It was as if a strong man were to seize a weaker man by the head and master, crush, and force him.

"By resolute effort, I achieved an unconfused mind, but my body was agitated and disturbed by such painful effort.

"Then I thought, what if I now practice trance without breathing? And I held the inbreathings and outbreathings of the mouth and nose, and there was an extraordinary roar in my ears. It was a roar like the bellows of a forge. But in the end, although my mind was unconfused, my body was painfully disturbed."

The years passed with such exercises. Gautama's clothes rotted. The birds perched on his head as he sat in motionless trance, and their droppings matted his hair. Sometimes he felt supreme joy rise in him, a religious joy, but this, like all other emotions, was unwelcome, for it had to be crushed. Fears plagued him too, induced by the dark mystery of the forest. He said to himself, "I will walk to and fro and not let myself stand until these fears have left me." But when he stood still, the fears returned. He thought, "I'll stand still and not let myself sit down until these fears have left me." But when he sat down, the fears returned. "I neither walked to and fro nor sat down nor lay down until I had overcome that fear and terror."

He lived on berries and weeds, or on what he occasionally begged in the town; sometimes the townsmen would bring him food as an act of merit. He tried starving himself. "I thought, what if I were to take only as much food as I can hold in my hollowed palm, beans or peas or lentils. And I took less and less food and became exceedingly thin. . . ."

The Buddhist artists, hardly able to bear the thought of their Teacher's miseries, rarely depict these years of his life, and the scribes disliked recording them. They invented an anxious angel who came down from heaven and threatened to feed him by divine means through his hair roots. But Gautama would not accept this kindly interference. He pointed out that if the angel did any such thing, all of his efforts would become a mockery and a lie. "Now enough!" he told the angel, and the angel fled.

"Like dried canes became my arms and legs, withered through this extremely scanty diet; like the feet of a camel became my buttock, like a string of beads my spinal column, like the roof-beams of an old house my sharply protruding ribs. And just as in a deep and narrow well the little stars of water below are hardly seen, so were my eyes in their sockets."

One day his hand slid to his belly, and he found himself grasping his spinal column. Feeling around his back for his spinal column, he touched his belly. In order to restore his strength a little, he chafed his limbs, and wherever he rubbed, skin and hair fell off.

Some townsmen came by, and one of them exclaimed, "The ascetic Gautama has turned black!" Another said, "No, he has turned brown!" and another said, "No, he has turned the color of a mangura-fish."

He was starving to death.

"What ascetic of the past has ever felt such a painful, burning, bitter sensation?" he asked himself. "This is the uttermost. Beyond this one cannot go." He recalled now that day of his boyhood when he had sat under a rose apple tree and sunk into a trance. What pure happiness had welled up in him then! His mind had enjoyed perfect communion with nature, his body was aloof from all pain. Could such happiness which does not come from desire or greed be considered evil? What was he doing here, thrusting spiritual happiness from him as if it were a black sin; and trying to conquer suffering while suffering acutely?

"Surely," he thought, "it is by happiness that one wins happiness!"

But despite his doubts, he persisted, for one does not throw away six years of effort in a single day.

One day as he sat in meditation, he fell over in a faint, and he lay there too weak to move. A goatherd passed by with his flock, and seeing the holy man inert on the ground, took the liberty of squeezing a little milk from a goat's udder into his mouth. Reviving somewhat, Gautama asked the boy to bring him a bowl of milk; but at this the goatherd shrank fearfully back and said, "Holy sir! Remember I am of low caste, and you will be defiled by food handed to you by me!"

"It is virtue, not caste, that decides excellence in man," replied Gautama. "Bring me a bowl of milk." Neither Gautama, nor the Buddhists who lived after him, ever had the slightest use for caste.

Revived by the goat's milk, Gautama remained in

meditation. Some dancing girls came by, and they were singing a song about a lute: if the lute was strung too loosely, it uttered dull noises; if it was strung too tightly, the noises were high and strained; but if it was strung properly, neither too loose nor too tight, beautiful music could be struck from it. This song carried a message to Gautama, and he took it to heart. He realized that never by fierce asceticism could he attain wisdom, any more than he could have attained it amid the luxuries of his princely palace. He resolved to have done with extremes and to find a Middle Path.

Another windfall came his way. There was in Uruvela a young wife named Sujata, and for a long time she had prayed for a child. Now a child was on its way, and as an act of gratitude, she decided to make an especially rich offering to the dreadful holy man who lived in the forest and who seemed to her, with his matted hair and burning eyes, to be the very genie of the place. She prepared a pudding made of the richest cream in which she boiled the finest rice, the grains picked over carefully so that each one was like a pearl. She sweetened the pudding with honey, spiced it, poured clear butter over it, and decorated it with flowers. Then she carried it to Gautama. To this day rice pudding is the Buddhist Staff of Life, and a common offering in temples.

Restored by the rice pudding, Gautama began to feel that he had now regained sufficient strength to go begging in the town, but he was naked and foul. He crept to the burial grounds where the poor laid their dead in shallow graves, and he gathered together some scraps of shrouds that had not been consumed by jackals. Painfully he washed them in the river Lilajan, and he washed himself too, dragging himself up and down the banks by means of overhanging branches. Somehow he managed to fasten his rags together, and clothing himself, he thereafter went into the town daily.

His health gradually returned and with it his beauty, so that the people of the town gasped in amazement, and the young girls' hearts beat, and they came trooping into the forest carrying lavish offerings in prettily decorated bowls.

But when Gautama's five companions who had been suffering privations in the wilderness emerged and saw him, they were thoroughly annoyed. "Behold the ascetic Gautama," they said. "He has given up. He has fallen into luxury."

In disgust they left him and went off in the direction of Benares, leaving Gautama alone.

# 5

# Enlightenment

*I knew a man, and whether he was in the body or out of it I cannot say, but he was caught up to the third heaven, caught into paradise, and heard unspeakable words which it is not lawful for a man to utter.*

ST. PAUL (II COR., 12, 2-4)

Gautama was now thirty-five years old, and it seemed to him that for all his years of earnest effort, he was no closer to achieving the wisdom he would need to deliver mankind from suffering than he had been before. But he was looking on the dark side: his strivings in the wilderness were by no means wasted. The teachings of Alara and Udraka would one day be incorporated into his "Higher Doctrine." What the yogis had taught him about trance—that mental state which comes about through intense concentration—would be used by the Buddhists as an instrument for the control of body, emotions, and mind.

For the present, Gautama's body, once health had been restored, was hardened and equal to any privation. Above all, he had spent six years exercising the remarkable gift he was born with: the power to reason. One cannot practice anything for so long without becoming good at it.

He now left the town of Uruvela and wandered aimlessly in the neighborhood for a while. He arrived at the spot we now call Bodh-Gaya.

Today Bodh-Gaya is a jumble of habitations built on ruins of habitations. The ground is stamped hard by feet of millions, billions, of pilgrims, tourists, and people who extort money from them. It is dotted with flower-decorated shrines which are 2,000-year-old heaps of dead flowers and rice pudding.

A narrow red tower, a sculptured pagoda, stands erect against the sky, 160 feet high, and at its base in a low enclosure made of bricks stands a choked tree of the kind the Indians call a pipal and the botanists call *Ficus religiosa*. It is the Indian fig, a relative of the banyan, and it has the faculty of sending down innumerable shoots from many branches, which grow until acre after acre is screened by its dark green leaves. When one trunk dies, there is always another to carry on life in a tree-genealogy that may continue for hundreds, thousands, of years.

The pipal of Bodh-Gaya is the Bo tree, the Tree of Wisdom; the most celebrated, and adored, certainly the most stared at, and the oldest historical tree in the world.

When Buddha first entered the shade of this tree, or rather that of its ancestor, it must have been already old. The region about him was a thicket or jungle, although it lay not far from the main route to Benares. He had been looking for a lonely spot where he could meditate undisturbed, and under the giant screen of this pipal, festooned with vines, he found it. He made himself a cushion out of grass and sat down facing the east in the lotus position, the primary yoga position of meditation. "Never from this seat will I stir until I have attained the supreme and absolute wisdom," he vowed to himself. Then he turned his schooled powers of concentration inward.

Step by step he retraced his mind's journey thus far through the realm of abstract thought. He grappled anew with every problem that had ever confronted him; examined afresh every observation, every thought or wisp of thought that might provide a key to the riddle of life. He forced himself to trace every argument to its intricate roots, and then to chase every paradox to its mathematical solution.

He was in a trance. Such prolonged and intense concentration is not possible in a normal state of mind. He was wandering down a narrow path toward a strait gate. Perhaps it is the same one Christians talk about when they say, "Knock and it shall be opened unto you; seek, and ye shall find."

The ancient tales do not agree about how long Gautama sat under the Bo tree; some of them say his vigil lasted seven weeks, and some say seven days. We are not told how he got nourishment or drink. We know that mystics in a trance state are able to endure long periods of time without food or drink, their pulse slow, their heartbeat hardly to be heard, their bodily needs and functions slowed almost to the point that they are entirely suspended.

It is therefore possible that Gautama sat for many days, even weeks, under the Bo tree.

He plunged through the successive levels of trance, past the realm of conscious reason into the dark corridors that lie below thought. The legend-makers have described with a wealth of poetic imagery how he met every possible emotion, felt it, fought with it, subdued it, disposed of it.

Mara came and tempted him. This oriental Satan had been hoping for some years that Gautama's erroneous thinking would do his work and lure his victim back to the princely luxury of Kapilavastu. He had been outraged when, upon abandoning his severe penances, Gautama had not gone home for a good meal but had taken only enough nourishment so that hunger could not interfere with his questing thought. Now Mara was desperate. He knew that his victim was in danger of escaping forever from his clutches.

And so he came and spoke to Gautama in alluring language about the pleasures of worldly dominion. He dangled fabulous treasure before his eyes, palaces and gardens, and he put on parade splendidly arrayed armies all walking in step in front of him. "Think how much good you could do if you were Chakravarti," he said slyly.

Gautama did not move.

Mara called forth his daughters. He arrayed them in the world's beauty and commanded them to go against

Gautama with every sorcery women can command. They pressed forward coquettishly, holding their veils over only half of their faces. They showed him the pearly garlands of their teeth. They yawned and threw up their dimpled arms. They moved their red lips. They smiled with their eyes half closed. They let slip their saris from their shoulders. They tightened their garments to show their slim waists. They jingled their ankle bells.

They walked and laughed, pretending not to notice Gautama, and then glanced over their shoulders and winked. Giggling, blushing, dancing, singing, they wriggled and turned, making sure that he saw every dainty lineament of their cheeks and bodies. Gautama sat calm as a lotus, sturdy as an elephant.

Mara's daughters lost heart. Truthfully, they were ashamed of themselves. Their victim had met their onslaught without passion and without reproach, gazing upon them with sublime understanding. They bent and kissed his feet before returning to Mara, and they said, "Father, he is gentle and surveys us as calmly as he surveys the mystery of heaven. Father, there was no conflict nor quarrel between us. He was kind. Father, change sides!"

But the Wicked One was not done with Gautama, not yet. He roared for his captains, the Sins. One by one he sent them against his victim: Selfishness, Hate, Greed, Ambition, Pride, Ignorance, Fear, Lust; the Thinker stared into their lurid faces one by one, and one by one they slunk away, knowing him to be their master.

Now Mara lifted up his sword and called upon his

captains, threw them in full force against Gautama with thunder, lightning, and globes of fire. He tore mountains asunder from the earth and hurled them at the Thinker, with floods of lava and molten iron spilling from their sides. From the deep abysses of the earth unthinkable monsters rose shrieking and fell upon him in violence and wrath.

Gautama sat walled in light. He knew this inky crew for what they were: sickly illusions. And gradually he was becoming aware of a reality. Wisdom exists. It is part of the human condition and has the same right to dominion on earth as Mara's hosts. In sudden triumph, with his right hand he struck the earth, calling upon it to bear witness to this fact; and the earth, trembling in response, opened up and swallowed the monstrosities that besieged him.

Mara picked up a reed and pensively wrote upon the ground: "The ascetic Gautama will escape my realm."

The light increased. Down the narrow path of spirit plunged the wandering beggar into the deep source where intuition dwells. His Buddha-eye was opening. He was clairvoyant. Now he saw the mystery of his own being explained. He was no prince, nor even an ascetic. He was a spark of energy that had been from the beginning. Through countless aeons he had wedded with every form of matter and animated a thousand lives; and finally he had become perfect. He was a Bodhisattva, and he was going to be enlightened.

With this expanded knowledge he surveyed the world of men in time and space, knew their thoughts, their feelings, their misery, and their grandeur. He felt again the godly compassion which was the sole reason for his existence. Ecstasy seized him; but he did not stir. Nothing could move him any more or stay his plummeting quest into the last trance where man meets heaven.

And now he was there, alone in the pure heart of things, utterly alone in space, almost alone in time, and still as stone. He brushed the door, it opened, a blinding radiance burst upon his mind, and the Universe smote him with its truth.

No storyteller of the past or present can prove with words or even understand a religious experience like this. It is conceivable only to the Thinker himself. And yet we cannot dismiss it as pure fantasy, because we know from other sources that mighty insight is possible to man.

Some such awesome splitting of the membrane which separates man from the infinite could have occurred on Mount Sinai, where Moses received Commandments upon which our system of law and ethics is based. Some sort of enlightenment stunned St. Paul on the road to Damascus, and he heard "unspeakable words." Mahomet, alone on the hillside above Mecca, was wisdom-struck. The lives of saints and prophets tell of men and women suddenly acquiring enormous knowledge.

Enlightenment of low degree happens to every one of us. We go to a strange city and the streets seem a meaningless tangle, but suddenly we can find our way about them. We learn a foreign language which is a jumble of words and idioms; but after a while we find ourselves speaking and understanding it. We study a certain subject which at first seems to be a chaos of unrelated facts. But there comes a time when, surveying our knowledge, we find that it forms a pattern which we comprehend.

The machinery of enlightenment exists in the human mind. We therefore cannot call the tale of the Great Enlightenment pure legend. Gautama was a man naturally gifted with intellect, and for years he had been using it to tackle the deepest riddles of human life. There came a point in his thinking when the pattern showed itself.

The truth that burst on Gautama under the Bo tree is one that cannot be proved or disproved. It is a matter of faith. At the bottom of his thinking he had various ideas which are quite foreign to us. Like all Hindus he believed in the transmigration of souls—the notion that after death the soul lives on to be reborn in another body; and that this happens over and over again. The kind of body, and the life it will lead, is determined by the Law of Karma. This is the arithmetic of the universe which totes up every person's good and bad deeds and thoughts. If good deeds and thoughts outweigh bad ones, the soul will be rewarded by good fortune in this life or the next. If bad deeds and thoughts prevail, misfortune is his lot.

Now Gautama saw in his compassion that all lives, even the most fortunate ones, are heirs to a good deal of misery. All bear a common burden of suffering: all endure sickness, old age, and death. It seemed to him that somewhere, somehow, there had been a general failure of goodness, so that the Law of Karma was weighing heavily upon every individual, and none escaped.

He wanted to discover what had started it all and then to conspire with mankind to put an end to this severe arithmetic; confound it with such goodness that it would stop, and mankind would be delivered to happiness, *Nirvana*.

And so, it is said that when he sat under the Bo tree, the true reason was given to him. It is ignorance. The soul chases after life ignorantly, the way a dog chases after the moving wheel of a motor car for a minute of foolish fun, not knowing its terrible danger, and ignoring the fact that it is really much happier when it is at rest.

Ignorance is the trigger that makes the soul run after life, because it gives rise to a huge burden of wrong desires. The wrong desires bring about awareness of Self, which in turn engenders self-love. When the soul loves, it begins to crave. No sooner does it crave than it grasps, and it grasps tangible things; for instance, life. Life brings inevitably in its train sorrow, sickness, old age, and death. Death brings rebirth and a repetition of the tragedy.

This is the Buddhist Chain of Causation. It sounds gloomy. Indeed, many people find that Gautama's teaching is too pessimistic to suit them. But these critics do not follow his thinking far enough. For sitting under the Bo tree, Buddha examined his theory backward and forward and upside down. Expressed in another way, the Chain of Causation reads: "If ignorance ceases, wrong desire ceases and so do selfish efforts, self-love, craving, grasping, rebirth, sorrow, sickness, old age, death." The

The Enlightened Buddha is often represented with a halo of
cobras, as in this Cambodian version from the Khmer Period
(12th century), a stone fragment found near Angkor Vat.
Shortly after the Enlightenment a great storm threatened to
disturb Buddha's meditations; but the Naga (Serpent) King
came out of his hole and seven times encircled the body of the
Blessed One, extending his immense hood as a shelter
over Buddha's head.

*Courtesy The Metropolitan Museum of Art*

soul then becomes perfect and is absorbed into the perfection of Nirvana.

"Ceasing, ceasing!" said Gautama. "At that thought, brethren, there arose in me a vision never taught before. A knowledge arose, insight arose, light arose."

That light would one day be called the Light of Asia: a majestic ethical system whereby man's wandering soul is given a goal: to perfect itself.

Gautama eventually got up from under the Bo tree and resumed his wandering in the neighborhood of Uruvela. He sat down under other trees while turning over and over in his mind a means of interpreting his ideas to men. The sheer magnitude of this task daunted him as the demoniac illusions of his trance had failed to do. He felt that even if he could find words to explain himself, this busy world would never pause in its running, never stand still and understand; and some, indeed, would not be capable of understanding.

Then an image occurred to him. He thought of a forest pool in which the lotus grows with its roots in the mud. Some plants, striving upward, do not reach the surface of the water and their heads remain submerged. Other plants reach the surface, barely, and float upon it. Still others thrust their heads above the water and flower in splendor. But all have their roots in the mud.

Reflecting on this, Gautama realized that there were many who stood ready and able to understand his teaching; others who would hear, but barely grasp it; and still others who would neither hear nor understand. And yet, all these multitudes strove upward, seeking light, because it was in their nature to do so.

Suddenly Buddha was seized with immense compassion for mankind, so helplessly rooted, so ceaselessly searching. This emotion streamed through him like the sap of a tree in spring; it was never to leave him but was to become the motivating force of his life, dissolving his self-doubts and strengthening him in his mission: that of a Buddha, an Enlightened One, a Teacher.

Shortly afterward, as he sat under a tree, some merchants on their way to Benares came upon him, and they fed him with rice and honey and gave him a new begging bowl. They were amazed at the benign power that seemed to shine forth from his person. They watched him eat their alms and clean his bowl, and they knelt to him reverently before they passed on their way, because he was transfigured and they knew that he had been blessed.

# 6

# The Wheel of Dharma

*To get rid of that "I am" conceit, this truly is the highest happiness.*

MAHAVAGGA

After the merchants had left him, Buddha remained for a while in the woods of Uruvela wondering where he ought to start his teaching and whom he should teach. He would have liked to begin with his old *gurus*, Alara and Udraka; they would have understood him readily, he knew. But both of them had died.

Students of Buddhism recognize—as did Gautama himself—that the ideas he was about to impart were original mainly in the way he said them; he had created a new standpoint which made it possible to draw new conclusions. While he was a man of exceptional mind, he was still the heir to the wisdom of many philosophers who had gone before him: the Vedic sages and the later sages whose thoughts had been preserved in the Hindu scriptures, the Upanishads. Alara and Udraka had profoundly influenced him, and there were many more philosophers of his day whose names we shall never know who were grappling, as Indian thinkers have always done, with the ultimate mysteries of God, the Universe, the soul, the Self, the will, the world, the good, the bad, the finite, the infinite, and so on.

Buddha's genius was that he not only heard the many voices of his land but he understood their common meaning. He systematized, simplified, and reconciled their discords. In doing this he brought the most advanced thought of his time out of the heads of the philosophers and into the service of man.

His fundamental notions were already tingling in his mind when he left Uruvela and went in search of the five disciples who had shared his years in the wilderness and then deserted him. When last seen they had been going in the direction of Benares, and so Buddha followed them by the same route the merchants had taken.

Benares was then, as it is now, the holy heart of Hinduism, a center of religious argument. As he approached, four miles north of the city he came to a deer park, Isipatana—a place now called Sarnath—where many ascetics and philosophers used to foregather under the trees, and it was here that Buddha's five former disciples were sitting skinnily upon the ground. They saw him coming, well-fed as he was on rice and honey cakes, and they were not pleased. "Here comes Gautama," they said, "fat and sleek, who has given up the struggle and reverted to large meals. Let's pretend not to notice him."

But he was coming straight toward them, and as he drew nearer they relented and said, "Well, let's make a place for him anyway." This is not the first legend or the last that leads us to suspect that Gautama Buddha was an extremely likable man.

By the time Buddha had come close to their group, the five had thrown their annoyance to the winds and came forward with joy to greet him; one took his bowl, another showed him a seat, another brought water for him to wash his feet. When he was comfortably seated and refreshed, they tackled him about their differences, addressing him as "friend."

"Brothers, don't call me friend," said Buddha. "Call me Truth-finder. For I have found it, brothers! Give ear to me! Let me teach you! Walk the path I show you and soon, even in this life, see for yourselves that incomparable goal of your holy life."

But the brothers were skeptical. "You did not see the higher vision when you practiced austerities, *friend* Gautama," they said. "How can you have seen it now that you are fat?"

"I am not fat," protested Buddha. "I am not lazy and I have not reverted to large meals. Listen to me! The immortal has been won! Let me teach you!"

Three times the brothers maintained that they had no patience with Buddha, and three times Buddha assured them that they would not regret listening to him. Finally he said, "Brothers, do you admit that I have never spoken to you in this way before this day?"

They were obliged to reply that even when practicing the holiest austerities, Gautama had never claimed wisdom or any right to teach them.

"Then give ear!" said Buddha, and he preached the

First Sermon in the deer park near Benares under the trees.

Buddhists call this event the "Setting in Motion of the Wheel of the Law"—the Dharma. Historians do not know for certain that his words to the five outlined his essential beliefs in such complete form as they have come down to us. But the text is ancient, and it has established the tradition that this First Sermon contained the very kernel of his system, the basic ideas common to all the far-flung Buddhist sects today.

The central truths that Buddha wanted the brothers to apply their minds to were the four truths about Suffering. It is a grim fact that human life suffers. Suffering begins with birth which inevitably brings in its train all sorts of ills: the loss of those we love, the presence of things we hate, the lack of what we want, illness, old age, and death; and the fears and anxieties brought about by all these. There is no use ignoring the hole gnawed by suffering in the center of oneself. The First Noble Truth is: SUFFERING EXISTS.

Next, he explained to them the Chain of Causation. We are continually plunged into this bath of suffering because of the soul's ignorant craving for life and the pleasures and passions of life. The Second Noble Truth is: SUFFERING IS CAUSED BY SELF-CENTERED DESIRE.

Once this cause is pinpointed, it follows that it can be renounced, subdued, destroyed. The Third Noble Truth is: SUFFERING CAN BE MADE TO CEASE.

Using these first three ideas as a springboard, Buddha now leapt from theory into practice. It is one of the most useful leaps a mind has ever taken. The Fourth Noble Truth is: SUFFERING IS MADE TO CEASE BY FOLLOWING THE NOBLE EIGHTFOLD PATH.

He then explained what he meant by the Noble Eightfold Path, taking the opportunity to make some pointed remarks about his reasons for giving up his self-torture at Uruvela.

"There are two extremes, brothers," he said, "which he who has given up the world ought to avoid. The one is a life given to pleasure. The other is a life given to mortification. The life given to pleasure is degrading, vulgar, and ignoble. The life given to mortification is painful, vain, and profitless.

"By avoiding these two extremes, brothers, I have gained the knowledge of the Middle Path which leads to wisdom, insight, calm, knowledge—in fact it leads *in this life* to happiness, salvation, Nirvana!

"What is this path? It is Eightfold. It consists of right views; right resolve; right speech; right action; right work; right effort; right mindfulness; and right concentration."

Many of these Buddhist commandments place emphasis upon an attitude of mind; this is because the Law of Karma takes into account one's thoughts and feelings as well as one's deeds. Right views means knowledge of the Four Noble Truths. Right resolve means the determination to renounce worldly pleasure and expunge malice from the mind. Right speech means no falsehood, back talk, harsh language, and frivolous gossip. Right action means no destroying life, no stealing, and no immorality. Right work means finding the honorable occupation that

The First Sermon. This famous statue is from the remarkable
ruins, dating from the 4th and 5th century, at Sarnath,
once the site of Isipatana deer park where, according to
the legend, Buddha gave his First Sermon.

*Courtesy Information Service of India*

fits one best. Right effort means bending the strength of mind and body toward following faithfully the Noble Eightfold Path. Right mindfulness means to become detached from thought of Self. Right concentration is meant for monks, and it means practicing the trance states in which man in this life experiences the tranquil happiness of Nirvana.

This was the practical teaching that was to march straight into the understanding of so many millions of people. The rules of the Eightfold Path are a guide for the perfection of character. It is true that absolute obedience is possible only to one who embraces totally the religious life—a monk or a nun; no one has ever pretended otherwise. But the ideal is clear to all: it marks out a way of life devoted to good and draws into the cosmic pattern all those who seek the balanced contentment which is the reward of simple virtue. Buddha said, "The man who can repeat little of the Teaching, but live it ... his lot is with the holy ones."

Buddha was to spend the rest of his life explaining his complex reasoning, defining such notions as "right" and "soul" and "self-centered desire." In his lifetime he stitched with dazzling threads the world of spirit to the world of action. For centuries after him Buddhist thinkers continued to build creatively on his ideas, and the sum total is what we call Buddhist philosophy, metaphysics, psychology.

This system of thought is taken on faith by the ordinary Buddhist. It is like the superb wing of a butterfly, necessary for higher flight; but the moral law is the body and the life.

In the deer park of Isipatana, the eldest of the five ascetics, Kondanya, was the first to recognize the quality of the Doctrine, to grasp it wholly. "Having penetrated the Dharma and having overcome uncertainty and doubt, having gained full knowledge and dependent upon nobody else for knowledge, he said to the Blessed One: 'Let me be a recluse under you, let me receive ordination.' "

Buddha then replied, "Come, monk. You have learned the Dharma well. Lead a holy life for the sake of the complete end of suffering."

The next members of the Order were Vaspa and Bhadrika. The remaining two ascetics, Mahanama and Assaji, proved a little more difficult to enlighten, and Buddha spent some days instructing them while the others went in search of food. It was in the course of this further instruction that Buddha delivered his second sermon. This one contains a teaching quite strange to our western way of thinking, but one that all Buddhists must take for granted if they expect to follow the Noble Eightfold Path. It is the doctrine of the "Not-Self."

As Buddha expressed it then and elaborated on it in the course of years, the teaching may be paraphrased like this:

"What is the Self? The body cannot be the Self because it is impermanent, changing always, constantly getting sick or well or tired or old. You cannot at any moment point to your body and say, 'This is myself.' If we admit that the body is not the Self, we are reduced to calling it a Not-Self.

"Your feelings are not your Self. They too are in a constant state of flux. What you feel now, you won't feel in a minute or two. Therefore it would be foolish to point to your feelings and say, 'This is myself.' The feelings are a Not-Self.

"Your thoughts are not your Self. They too are impermanent, and what you think now is not what you have thought before or will think in the future. Thoughts are a Not-Self.

"The soul is not a Self. How can it be when it is in a permanent state of becoming? It becomes a better soul when you live a good life, and a worse soul when you lead an evil one. The soul, therefore, is a Not-Self.

"What about all these things together? Are they the Self? No, because since each one is constantly changing, their relationships are constantly changing.

"In short, you are not a Self. You are just a bundle of Not-Selves. Stop thinking about your Self."

Buddha, when he put his mind to it, could easily prove to people that they were not really there, and he did not hesitate to do so, because he had a lively sense of humor. But his main purpose in this teaching—besides wanting to hear a little less about Self—was to bring home to his disciples the pathetic perishability of what they held dearest—themselves—and oblige them to look deeper, for a more stable object of admiration.

"Does that which is perishable cause pain or joy?"

"It causes pain, lord."

"And is it possible to say of a thing that is perishable, painful, subject to change, 'This is mine, this is me, this is myself'?"

"Impossible, lord."

"Considering this, monks, the wise disciple turns away

from the body, from feelings, perception, soul, mind.
Turning away, he loses passion and losing passion he is
liberated."

The Hindu thinkers of Buddha's day, no less than
western students of ours, were bothered by Buddha's
disrespectful attitude to the soul, which most Hindus
believe to be a fragment of the "Eternal," and we call
"immortal."

Buddha was a philosopher, though, and as a philosopher he could not put forward the thought that everything in the Universe was in a state of frantic motion
and change, without being forced to affirm that somewhere there was a Norm, a changeless thing to measure
by.

For Buddha, that still Norm was not the soul, but the
soul's goal: happiness, liberation, Nirvana.

In the city of Benares at that time there lived a
spoiled young man named Yasa who had rolled in luxury
all his life and had never done a hard day's work. He
was bored. One day at dawn, unable to sleep, he rose
from his bed, left his father's fine house, and went for a
stroll in the deer park Isipatana. Buddha was awake and
saw him coming: he could hardly have overlooked him,
because Yasa was wearing golden slippers of quite unusual shape. As he walked he kept saying to himself,
"Oh dear! Oh dear! What a bother!"

Buddha said, "Come and sit down by me. There's no
bother here."

Yasa sat down, and Buddha began to tell him about
the Dharma, laying special stress on morals, the sinful-

ness of desire, and the blessings of becoming detached from Self. He made no swift impression on Yasa.

In the meanwhile, Yasa's mother had become uneasy, as mothers do when they scent a crisis. Finding that her son had run away from home, she woke her husband who, after sending messengers to the four corners of the earth, turned his own steps to the deer park where he quickly saw the unusual marks of Yasa's golden slippers in the dust. When Buddha saw the father approaching, he exerted his magic powers to make Yasa invisible, slippers and all. The father, drawing near, said, "Pray, holy one, have you seen a young man wandering about?" Buddha replied, "Why not sit down here? Perhaps if you sit here, you will see him sitting here also."

Not knowing quite what to make of this but glad of a rest, the father did so; and for some time thereafter Buddha lectured him about the Four Noble Truths and the Eightfold Path. Yasa's father became deeply attentive; he realized that he was sitting next to a great man, and concentrating intently upon everything that Buddha was saying, he penetrated the teaching and understood it.

"Glorious lord, glorious lord!" he exclaimed. "Just as if one should set up what had been overturned, or reveal what had been hidden, or point out the way to someone lost, or bring a lamp into the darkness, so has your Doctrine reached my mind!

"I take my refuge in the Buddha. I take my refuge in the Doctrine. I take my refuge in the Order. May the Blessed One receive me from this day forth while my life lasts as a lay disciple who has taken refuge!"

Yasa's father thus became the first lay Buddhist.

All this while the invisible Yasa had been listening to Buddha and ideas were revolving rapidly in his mind. Now Buddha ceased to exert his magical power and Yasa became visible. "My son," said his father, "your mother is mourning and grieving. Go home and give life to your mother!"

But Yasa was not ready to go home. He had glimpsed a purpose for his life and he meant to stay and hear more of it. Understanding how he felt, Buddha persuaded the father to permit Yasa to remain, promising to bring him home by lunchtime.

When the father had gone, he continued to talk to the young man, and "as a clean cloth free from black specks properly takes the dye," Yasa drank in the Dharma. He begged Buddha to let him remain with him and become a monk. He was the sixth disciple.

At noon Buddha and his new disciple went to Yasa's house where his mother and wife had been busy preparing exceptionally delicate food for the holy man. What a change they saw in Yasa! Instead of sulky looks, he had a calm mien, and he was listening seriously to someone for a change. The women realized that Buddha was responsible, and they came forward themselves to listen to the teaching. Afterward, they asked if they too might become lay disciples.

In short, Yasa and his family proved to be the most zealous early Buddhist missionaries. No less than fifty-four of their friends and relations left their homes to follow Buddha.

# 7

# The Samgha

*O Joy! We live in bliss; amongst men of hate, hating
none. Let us indeed dwell among them without hatred!*

DHAMMAPADA

We need not cast much doubt on the legends that tell
how rapidly the Wheel of Dharma rolled from the
moment Buddha set it in motion; we know historically
that Buddhism had remarkable spreading power. The
first sixty disciples were the nucleus of the Samgha, that
famous body of yellow-clad monks which is still active
in many countries—the oldest, most widespread, con-
tinuously organized body of men in the world.

The legends—and those covering the second half of
Buddha's life seem to have real historical foundation—
imply that success took him by surprise. He does not
appear to have seen himself as the leader of a veritable
horde of monks, but rather as a wandering holy man
with a band of intellectual lotuses to exhort and instruct,
who would have no other shelter than a tree, no other
seat than the earth. In such a way they lived at first
at Isipatana.

But the Samgha quickly outstripped all reasonable expectations. Apart from the inherent beauty and common sense of the Dharma itself, this can only have been due to the compelling personality of Gautama Buddha, comparable only to that of Jesus who could make people drop the tools of their trade to follow Him. Gautama was said to have had a manner "welcoming, friendly, polite, not frowning, speaking plainly and willingly."

Not long after the Yasa episode, Buddha journeyed alone to Uruvela and along the way in a woods he met thirty rich young men. They had been enjoying a picnic with their wives; but one of them who was not married had brought along a woman of low morals, and when the young men took off their ornaments and rich garments to go for a swim, she gathered up these articles and made off with them. They were running hither and thither in search of the thief when they came upon Buddha under a tree. "Now what think you, young men," asked the sage when he had learned the reason for the hullabaloo, "is it better for you to go in search of the woman, or to go in search of yourselves?"

The young men had to admit that they ought to be searching for themselves; and being well brought up they also had to sit and listen to Buddha. By the time he had finished with them they were members of the Samgha.

Buddha then proceeded to Uruvela where three renowned brothers named Kasyapa were living. They were worshipers of Agni, the Vedic fire god, and between them they led one thousand disciples. So profoundly was the eldest Kasyapa impressed by some magic tricks the way-

farer performed for him that when Buddha asked him
for lodging he impulsively consented to share his hut.
Afterward, he regretted his generosity: he remembered
that the Day of the Great Fire Sacrifice was at hand
when the people of Magadha would come in crowds to
watch his spectacular sacrifice, bringing with them offerings of food. Kasyapa was worried that if they were ex-
posed to Buddha's miracles, they might easily give their
offerings to him instead, and his own gain and honor
would diminish. "I hope he stays away from the feast,"
thought Kasyapa.

Buddha read his thought. On the great day he took
himself off to a nearby village where he begged his food
and ate it alone in the woods. The next day Kasyapa
came looking for him. "Where have you been? Why
didn't you come to the feast yesterday? We were thinking of you and we even set forth your portion."

Buddha replied, "Kasyapa, did you not hope that I
would stay away?" Kasyapa confessed to his shame that
the unworthy thought had entered his mind.

Kasyapa was proud and stubborn, but in the end he
fell into Buddha's net, and so did his brothers. They
and their thousand disciples cut off their hair and beards
and flung them into the river together with their fire-
worshiping utensils.

Now Buddha had one thousand and ninety-three disciples, every one of them eager to communicate his
teaching to others. When he had given them sufficient
instruction in the methodical pursuit of the Eightfold
Path, he taught them the eight qualifications of the mis-

sionary: he must be able to hear, and to make others listen; able to learn, to remember, and understand, and to make others understand; he must be skillful in dealing with foes as well as friends, and he must be no maker of quarrels. With this he sent them out across the Ganges Valley, saying, "A great duty is yours—to work for the happiness of men. Let us separate and go each in a different direction, no two following the same path—and preach the Dharma."

This missionary spirit remained characteristic of Buddhist monks until about A.D. 1000.

Buddha was a born organizer, and he now had the task of devising rules whereby he might manage these monks and inject them with his own vitality. He had to give up his ideal of total houselessness; there had to be a place where the monks could foregather, learn, and meditate upon what they had learned. Besides, after the rainy season it became apparent that his "Mob of Beggars," as he called them, had raised the ire of the populace. "How can the followers of the holy Sakya go on their travels alike during the winter, summer, and the rainy season?" many people asked. "They crush the green herbs, they hurt vegetable life, they destroy the lives of many small things."

When this complaint came to the ears of Buddha, he acquiesced: "I prescribe, monks, that you enter upon retreat in the rains."

Thereafter for three months of the year the monks would come together under shelter. The first of these monasteries was presented to them by King Bimbasara of Magadha. As Buddha's fame spread, this king had become curious about the son of the Sakyas who preached "a doctrine lovely in the beginning, lovely in the middle, and lovely in the end, in the spirit and in the letter." When Buddha wandered in the direction of his capital at Rajagriha the king visited him in a grove where he was dumfounded to find the sage packed tightly around with the stiff-necked Kasyapas and their disciples.

The king asked for instruction and received it. When Buddha had finished, Bimbasara said, "In former days, lord, when I was a prince, I had five hopes. The first was 'Oh, that I might be king!' This is now fulfilled. The second was, 'And then might a holy one, a fully En-lightened One, come into my kingdom!' This is now ful-filled. The third was, 'And that I might minister to that Blessed One!' That is now fulfilled. The fourth was, 'And might he, the Blessed One, preach his Dharma to me!' This is now fulfilled. The fifth was, 'And might I under-stand it.' That is now fulfilled."

With these gracious words the king asked to be received as a lay disciple, and he presented the brothers with a bamboo grove, Veluvana, which was "not too far from town and not too near, suitable for going and coming." There seems to have been some sort of shelter there, or else shelter was built for them by Bimbasara. In time other monasteries were raised by the generosity of the devout. They were groves enclosed by a wall with a gate. Small cells were provided for the monks, and a larger place for the superior where he could give instruction. There had to be plenty of shade trees about, and a running brook to carry away waste without killing fish; and the monastery could own such properties as brooms, slop basins, waterpots, and towels for the washing of the feet.

The rules for joining the Samgha were the simplest: one had to be twenty and honestly wish to learn the Dharma. At first Buddha received all aspirants and ordained them. But as the young men flocked into his fold and monks came limping back from all directions bringing converts with blistered feet, Buddha passed on his power of ordination to all monks, and he prescribed the ceremony himself:

"You ought, monks, to confer ordination in this way: let the novice first have his hair and beard cut off; let him put on yellow robes, and adjust his upper robe so as to cover one shoulder; let him salute the feet of the monks with his head and sit down squatting; then let him raise his joined hands and say three times over:

> 'I take my refuge in the Buddha
> I take my refuge in the Dharma
> I take my refuge in the Samgha.' "

This formula is known as the "Three Refuges" and it is the same that Yasa's father had used; and the same with which monks and lay Buddhists affirm their faith today.

Every monk took vows of poverty, celibacy, and harmlessness. He was allowed possession of the clothes he stood up in and an extra garment—and these had to be made out of rags picked from rubbish heaps, washed clean, and sewn together to make a sort of toga which covered the entire body except for the right shoulder. It was dyed saffron-yellow.

The reason for the choice of color is obscure. The yellow clothes Buddha is said to have exchanged with a huntsman is perhaps a historical clue. The theory has been advanced, also, that yellow blends modestly with the yellowish dust and mud of India, but this seems nonsense, since the saffron-robed monks stand out anywhere like walking sunspots. Buddha might well have chosen the color because he wanted his monks to be noticed. A flair for showmanship was certainly not contrary to the character of the "historical Buddha."

Besides his clothes, a monk might own a bowl, a needle, a razor to shave his head, and a filter to strain his drinking water—not for hygienic reasons, but to avoid the accidental slaughter of small insects. For the same humane motive he was allowed, when at a monastery, to have a narrow wooden bed slightly raised from the ground, to prevent him from crushing ants in his sleep.

He could eat only one meal a day and that before noon, and he was to obtain his food by begging scraps from householders. "As a bee takes honey from flowers without hurt to bloom or scent, so let the sage seek his food from house to house," said Buddha.

He was not to let himself notice whether the house was a prosperous or a poor one. By the Law of Karma the householder would acquire merit by giving him food, and the poorest therefore were to be given the same opportunity as the rich. He was to stand modestly beside door or window with his begging bowl, and if no food was offered to him, he was to pass on, permitting no unkind thought to arise in his mind.

If a woman gave him food he was not to observe whether she was old or young or comely—in fact, he was not to observe anything more than a plow's length in front of him, nor let himself be distracted by sounds or smells. His sense organs had to be fully controlled, for it was by such channels that wicked stimuli entered and tempted the mind from the Path.

For a monk of the Samgha, there was no standing about in street crowds watching jugglers and snake charmers. Nor could he receive money or listen to people who wanted him to come and have a drink.

He might accept an invitation to lunch from the faithful, but he must eat what was put before him and never conspire with his host to serve him his favorite food. Still, Buddha said, "A monk who has reached the fruition of spiritual welfare and the gladness attendant thereon . . . who has reached a pitch of virtue, character, and learning, may, without harm or hurt, eat the choicest rice with all manner of sauces and curries."

Of course, Buddha's object in saying this was not to condone hearty meals. He wanted to show that such food in the mouth of a very holy monk would at once be spiritually purified of any taste or taint of luxury. However that may be, this attitude left the way clear for shamelessly good cooking to flourish in many Buddhist countries, as it still does, for the benefit of us all.

No such dialectical blessing was applied in the matter

of celibacy. A monk might leave the Samgha at will, if
he felt he would be better off married. But a practicing
monk had to stay away from women.

"How should we behave to women, lord?"

"Not see them."

"And if we have to see them?"

"Not speak to them."

"And if we have to speak to them?"

"Keep awake!"

Once a beautiful courtesan fell in love with one of
Buddha's monks, and she sent word to him that she
wished to receive him at her house. He returned the
message, "The time for me to visit you has not yet arrived."

Thinking that he might be ashamed of his poverty, she
again sent word, assuring him that love and not greed
for gifts had prompted her invitation. Again he replied,
"The time for me to visit you has not yet arrived."

Now the courtesan committed a heinous crime: she
caused a traveling merchant to be murdered and stole
his property. The deed came to light, and she was tried
and condemned: her nose, hands, and feet were cut off
and she was thrown on the dunghill to die. Then the
monk came to her and said, "Now the time for me to
visit you has arrived." With her maid he tended her,
comforted and instructed her, and she became a lay disciple.

When at their morning begging, or on the road, the
monks had to be ready at all times to preach the Dharma—
using Buddha's own words which they had learned by
heart—to anyone who wanted to hear. Sometimes in the

texts, the phrase "returning thanks"—that is for a gift of food—is used to mean "giving a discourse."

At the monastery they cultivated the eighth step of the Path: Right Concentration. This was the practice of trance. One form of trance was simply controlled meditation in which the monk joyously contemplated the Universe, pouring out blessings on it—a sort of thought-song of good will.

Another sort of trance was the Dyana, a term more familiar to us in its Japanese form, Zen. This was an intellectual effort similar to Buddha's Enlightenment. The monk, by intense concentration, achieved such complete mechanical control of his thoughts that he could blot them out completely. Below the realm of consciousness, he gained control of his emotions and senses, and blotted them out too. On the level where intuition ruled his mind, he disposed of that also. Finally, sublime ecstasy arose, and when it subsided he had reached the incomparable end-of-the-Path, the calm haven of Nirvana.

Habitual practice of Dyana brought about equanimity of spirit, freedom from all craving, and an attitude of friendly detachment from the world.

It was recognized that not everybody could achieve the deep trance. Those who did were called *Aharats*, saints, and were said to be "enlightened," and exempt from rebirth. Other brothers struggled with their Right Views and Right Efforts all their lives long; but honesty of purpose was prized by Buddha, and there was room in the Samgha for all who struggled.

One day, not long after the First Sermon, an extremely

intelligent ascetic, a Brahmin named Sariputra, noticed one of Buddha's mob begging in the street, and he was much struck by the expression of serenity on his face. After having waited politely for the monk to fill his bowl, he accosted him and asked him to discourse on the new Dharma.

The monk, who happened to be one of the first five disciples, Assaji, replied rather modestly that he had not the eloquence to teach. However, he said that his Master's teaching could be summed up by the phrase: "Everything that has a beginning has an end."

This is a philosophical nutshell. It contains Buddha's idea that everything in this mortal universe is in frantic motion, caught in the swift mill of cause and effect. He reasoned that anything that has started to move must someday cease to move. He did not believe in perpetual motion, any more than a modern engineer does.

Sariputra saw the point at once. Thanking Assaji, he made haste to communicate this teaching to his close friend, Mogallana. These two, it is said, were born on the same day, grew up together, and left their homes together in search of a doctrine that could engross their excellent minds.

Now they came to Gautama who immediately recognized their ability. Since he was at that time engaged in organizing the Samgha, he placed them next to him in authority over his monks. The pair became among the most famous personalities—probably historic—who surrounded Buddha. Sariputra excelled in learning and in teaching. He is thought to have devised the system used

in the Samgha for explaining Buddha's teachings pain-
lessly to the slowest monks. Mogallana became an adept
of *iddhi*, the psychic powers that are said to be a by-
product of the practice of trance.

As the Samgha grew, grumbling was heard from the
population: "Gautama causes parents to be childless,
wives to become widows, and he causes the uprooting of
families. Too many distinguished clansmen are leading
the holy life with Gautama."

Buddha told his monks: "This noise will not last long.
It will die down. If people chide you, reply, 'It is truly
by a good Dharma that the Truth-finder leads us. Who
murmurs against the wise? Who grudges righteous leadership to the wise?' "

Buddha was right, the noise died. Still, he was creating
a problem. The Samgha was egalitarian, accepting men
of any and all conditions, castes, classes, or occupations.
Nevertheless, large numbers of young Kshatriya, the
flower of the land, were flocking to Buddha: soldiers,
noblemen, landowners. These were prosperous and well-
educated men, even though some of them did do their
own plowing.

In Buddha's time, a discrepancy had arisen in upper
class Indian customs. As has happened in other societies,
before and since, the minds of literate, well-to-do young
men had been aroused in sophisticated circles; and as a
result they no longer had the patience for the rough work
of farming or the utter physical devotion that their fore-
fathers had given to the land. How much better, the young

men thought, to live the gypsy life under the wing of a man who was an aristocrat like themselves, possessed of unending warmth and enormous intellectual power.

Their riches did not detain them. Riches are a very good thing if you know that you can keep them and pass them on to your children. But times were uneasy. The tribes to which these young Kshatriya belonged were continually at each other's throats with petty quarrels over fishing rights or forest rights or boundary rights, and these quarrels often became bloody massacres. Also the tribes were feeling the threat of Magadha's ambition. Their forebodings proved correct, for in the near future Magadha was to subjugate the lesser states, and the tribes would be ground to dust in the mill of history.

And so the noblemen joined Buddha and begged for a living with no feeling of loss of prestige, for they were expected to shine before the world as the image of the ideal man, the sage, the thinker. "Let there be no falling back in your aim," Buddha told them, "while there is something further to be done. And what is there further to be done? First to become conscientious and scrupulous; thereafter to become pure in deed, speech, thought, and mode of living; to become guarded as to the senses; to become moderate in eating; to become mindful and circumspect; to become possessed of the superior wisdom. Each of these is something further to be done."

Armed with this moral ideal, they went out with their begging bowls, and when they met with a hostile reception, they took strength from it. Not only did their vow of harmlessness forbid them to defend themselves by brawn; even angry thoughts had to be turned into sweet ones by trained spiritual force. "Wherefore, if anyone abuses you to your face or strikes you with his fist or throws clods of earth at you, or beats you, or gives you a blow with a sword—say to yourself, 'My heart shall be unwavering. No evil word will I send forth. I will abide compassionate of others' welfare, of kindly heart, without resentment.'"

By and by the people of the Ganges Valley became used to the "Mob of Beggars," and we are filled with admiration at their generosity, not only to Buddhist monks, but to those of other sects.

# 8

# Home to Kapilavastu

*Hard it is to leave home; hard also to live at home; hard is community life; to be a wanderer is also hard.*

DHAMMAPADA

By the time Gautama Buddha had been turning the Wheel of Dharma for three years he was the most renowned teacher of his day, rivaled only by Mahavira, "The Great Hero," leader of the Jains, whose opinions were similar to his own, but marred by extremism. Mahavira, for example, made his disciples go naked, saying that clothes were a useless vanity and an obstacle in the holy life.

Gautama was devoting his great energy to missionary activity, traveling through the lands of all the tribes—the Koliyas, the Mallas, the Vajjis, the Kasis, and so on; but he did not enter the domain of the Sakyas. He was known up and down the Ganges Valley as Sakyamuni—the Sakya Sage—but his tribe had not seen him for almost ten years.

Suddhodana yearned for sight of his son, and when he learned that Buddha had come to a temporary halt at Rajagriha, he sent messengers to invite him home. The found Buddha preaching to a large crowd. After listening to him for a while they joined the Samgha. Since monks entering the Path become immediately detached from matters of worldly interest, Suddhodana's message slipped out of their minds.

Nine times the king sent trusty messengers and nine times they deserted him for the Samgha. At last Suddhodana sent a childhood playmate of Siddhartha's called Udayin the Black. Like the rest Udayin entered the Order, but after two months he managed to recollect why he had come. Since the rains were over and the time for traveling had arrived, he recited a poem of sixty stanzas to Buddha, mostly in praise of nature, but hidden in the middle was one verse containing reference to the Master's family.

Buddha understood. He left for Kapilavastu at once with a company of monks.

As we know from another source, a prophet is without honor in his own country. Indeed it is not reasonable to expect people to fall down and worship someone they have known as a dusty boy. The Sakyas behaved no better than the Nazarenes. While they prepared a pleasant grove for Gautama, called Nigrodha, and brought him flower garlands as they would for anyone, they did not permit themselves to be impressed. Even after Buddha rose into the air and delivered to them a discourse from this vantage point, they remained stubborn. They took leave of him without so much as inviting him to come and beg at their doors.

The father made obeisance to him, though not without grudge. Suddhodana's fortunes had not prospered since Siddhartha had left home. He was at constant loggerheads with the powerful Prasenajit, king of Kosala, and getting the worst of it. He loved his son; but he loved even more the son of his imagination, who was a Universal Monarch and not a harmless wandering beggar.

The following day, Buddha took his begging bowl and went about the town from house to house. A window opened in a great palace and Yasodhara looked down on him. She immediately informed King Suddhodana who with agitated heart ran into the street after his son, expostulating: "Why are you disgracing our family in this way?"

"It is our custom, O king," replied Buddha.

"Our custom! We are Kshatriya of ancient lineage, and Kshatriya do not beg in the street!"

"That royal lineage is yours, O king," replied Buddha. "Mine is the Buddha-lineage of Dipankara and those who went before him. They gained their livelihood by begging."

There in the streets Gautama lectured his father, made him see how possessive love is but a greed of the mind which inevitably brings suffering in its wake. As his son spoke, the knot of resentment and vanity that had tormented Suddhodana loosened; his mind touched the Path, and perhaps he sensed that after all he was the father of a world-conqueror. Silently he took Buddha's begging bowl out of his hands and led him home.

So far Buddha had not come face to face with Yasodhara, and he was now told the reason: she had refused to come to him. "If I have any excellence, my master will come himself to me," she said, "and when he comes I will reverence him."

Buddha said, "She is not to be blamed," and he went to her apartments accompanied by two monks, according to a monastic rule that forbade a monk to be alone with a lady; but he told his companions that in spite of monastic rules if Yasodhara attempted to embrace him, she should be permitted to do so.

When Yasodhara saw him entering her rooms, she was overcome with emotion. She sank to the floor, clasped his ankles, and placed her head between his feet. Suddhodana said, "Lord, when my daughter heard that you were wearing yellow robes, she put on yellow robes; when she heard of your having one meal a day, she herself took one meal; when she knew that you lay on a narrow bed, she lay on a narrow bed; and when she heard that you had given up garlands and scents, she gave them up."

For all that, there was bitterness in the heart of Yasodhara, and she did not present Rahula to him at that visit. Her father never forgave Buddha his abandonment of her. He became a drunkard, and used to stand in Buddha's path cursing him.

The heir apparent of the kingdom of the Sakyas was not Rahula but Nanda, Buddha's half brother. He was the son of Prajapati, Buddha's foster mother and King Suddhodana's second wife. Two days after Buddha's arrival at Kapilavastu a festival was held in Nanda's honor, not only to celebrate his consecration as heir to the throne, but also his wedding to the most beautiful girl in the country.

Buddha came to see the happy pair as if paying a visit of congratulation and negligently gave Nanda his begging bowl to hold. After a little he rose, blessed the couple, and departed without taking back the bowl. Nanda thought he might be considered impolite if he reminded the great man of his forgetfulness, and so, over the objections of his bride, he followed Buddha back to the Nigrodha Grove, wearing his wedding clothes and carrying a begging bowl. Buddha turned and surveyed him. "I see you want to leave the world," he said.

Nanda thought it might sound impolite to say No, and so he said Yes. He was ordained then and there.

The boy Rahula was now about nine years old, fully alive to the excitement in the household due to the visit of the strange holy man. One day his mother called him, dressed him in his best, and told him to go and ask his father for his inheritance.

"Who is my father?" asked Rahula. "I know of no father except the king."

Yasodhara picked him up and held him to the window; below in the garden under a tree Buddha was taking his meal surrounded by monks and Sakyas. "That golden-colored monk is your father," she said. "Once he had four great vases of treasure, but since he left the world we do not see them. Go, Rahula, and tell him that you are a prince, and when you become a king you will have need of this wealth. Ask him to give you your inheritance."

Rahula went into the garden and wormed through the crowd until he stood at Buddha's side, but he did not dare to address his father. Buddha became aware of the small figure stationed next to him and looked around. Rahula thought quickly. "Your shadow, lord, is pleasant," he said.

Having finished his meal, Buddha rose up to return to the grove and Rahula followed close behind. Presently Rahula plucked up his courage, and when Buddha again looked around he said, "Give me my inheritance, holy one." Buddha said nothing.

As they proceeded farther away from the palace Rahula kept repeating his plea with more urgency. Buddha's attendant monks would have liked to stop him, but since Buddha said nothing they were silent. Gautama in fact was meditating upon the problem of Rahula. "This wealth he is asking for," he thought, "brings vexation with it. I will give him the nobler wealth I acquired under the Bo tree. I will make him the heir of a spiritual inheritance."

When they arrived at the grove and Rahula once again asked for his inheritance, Buddha turned to Sariputra and said, "Ordain him!"

Thus Rahula became an aspirant, and when he was twenty he was ordained a monk. Of course, Buddha had thousands of sons—he used to tell his monks that he considered himself their father. But perhaps the fact that some of Buddha's surviving discourses are addressed to one named Rahula suggests that he kept a place near to him for the son of Yasodhara.

There is no use trying to defend Buddha from the charge of being inconsiderate in snatching Nanda from his bride; and from the long-suffering king, his remaining heir, Rahula. None of the great religious teachers was ever considerate of worldly matters when it came to saving souls.

Suddhodana, however, was exceedingly sorrowful, and

he went to Nigrodha to reprove his son. "When you abandoned the world," he said, "it was a pain to me; and so it was when Nanda did so; and it is especially so in the case of Rahula. The love of a son cuts through the skin, and having cut through the skin it cuts through the flesh, the sinew, the bone, the marrow. Grant, lord, that the monks may not ordain a son without the permission of his mother and father."

Out of compassion for his father, Gautama formulated a rule that holds fast in the Samgha to this day: no one may enter the Order without the permission of parents, while they live.

It was now time for Buddha to take leave of his family, and with a company vastly increased by converted Sakyas, he set out on the return journey to Rajagriha.

When he had gone some distance, he was hailed from behind by Sakya noblemen headed by his two cousins, childhood friends and rivals for Yasodhara's hand, Ananda and Devadatta. All of them wished to enter the Order. Since they had not thought it right to appear on the public road without their jewelry, they had brought along their trusty barber, Upali, for the specific purpose of carrying this rich treasure back to Kapilavastu. A bundle was therefore made, and Upali shouldered it and set out for home. But after he had gone a little way, he began to wonder why. If the Samgha had no regard for caste or class, why should not he, a barber, enter it also? He hung his bundle on a tree and hastened back to Buddha.

Ananda, Devadatta, and the rest behaved extremely well, congratulating Upali on his decision. They seized the opportunity to demonstrate humility by insisting that Upali should be ordained before all of them, and thus acquire seniority in the Order. This was done, and in the course of time Upali, a man of considerable intellect, became one of the most important leaders of the Samgha.

Buddha was delighted to have his cousins with him. Ananda was to become his favorite disciple, his companion, confidant, secretary, and friend.

Shortly after his return to Rajagriha, Buddha made a most useful convert in a rich merchant, a man so famed for charity that he was called Anathapindaka, which means "giver of alms to the unprotected." The merchant came from Sravasti, the capital of Kosala—a town which has now been identified with Saheth-Maheth, an archaeological site on the river Rapti, near Faizabad. He invited Buddha to spend his next retreat at his city, and the sage accepted with the words: "The Order takes pleasure in empty dwelling places."

"Commanded, lord, commanded!" replied Anathapindaka, but when he returned home he did not bother to look around for an old house in which to shelter the monks. Instead he acquired a beautiful quiet park for which he paid a huge price: it is said that the owner demanded that every inch of the area be covered by a carpet of gold pieces down to the last square foot. On it he built the famous Jetavana Monastery.

Another monastery, Pubbarama, was built at Sravasti by an immensely rich lay disciple, a lady named Visakha, who could never stop thinking of good deeds to do for the monks. Her highest ambition was that when any monk was fortunate enough to enter Nirvana, he should have been helped on his way at Pubbarama where he would have had food, medicine, and a special robe for the rains, at her expense.

Some scholars believe that the legends of the munificent disciples of Sravasti are pure invention, written a long time after Buddha died by monks who wished to encourage monastery-building and gift-giving among the faithful by showing that the Teacher himself approved of such gifts.

The matter cannot be settled here. But the legends are very old, and the monasteries of Jetavana and Pubbarama must surely have existed, for they were the favorite residences of Buddha who spent his last twenty rainy seasons at one or the other of them.

Buddha was never an extremist in any practical issue. He seems to have given permission to his monks to accept bolts of cloth rather than waste their time at rubbish heaps. But they still had to tear it in strips small enough so that it had no value, and sew it up again. Medicine and robes for the heavy rains might have appealed to him as health measures. And the food mentioned as being provided by Visakha was not extravagant food: it was gruel.

Buddha had a mild streak, there is no doubt about that. He was no glaring ascetic, but an expansive and flexible man. There was only one subject upon which he was immovable as any man of principle must be: Nirvana, and the necessity of arriving there.

# 9

# The Lord Buddha:
## THE SAGE

*Then the blind men began to quarrel, saying, "Yes! No!
An elephant is not like that! Yes, it is like that!" And
the raja laughed.*

UDANA

After the story of the visit to Kapilavastu and the
founding of the Jetavana Monastery about 525 B.C., the
narrative sequence of the Buddha-legend ceases, and it
does not take up the thread of a story until forty-five
years later when Gautama was about to die.

Multitudes of tales tell what he did during this time,
but not in what order he did them. We know what he
said, taught, and thought, but not how his ideas developed.
They repose full-formed in the Buddhist scriptures,
glowing with a sense of the man he was—profound and
humorous, assertive and yet forbearing, a demanding but
considerate Teacher, a formidable logician and debater,
a mystic whose mind cut through fuzzy thinking like an
accurate piercing beam.

We do not know what he looked like. The main physical feature mentioned in the texts—apart from his

magical birthmarks—is the golden color of his skin. This accords with his probable race: the Sakyas must have been closely related to the Nepalese, a people with much Mongoloid blood, but still Indians, descendants of the light-skinned Aryans who dominated northern India in 3000 B.C.; and of the dark-skinned tribes the Aryans fought, conquered, and married.

Buddha had no interest in personal appearance. He instructed his followers to represent him in art by the symbol of the Bo tree. The oldest Buddhist sculptures at Sanchi, Bharhut, and Bodh-Gaya show that the artists had improved upon this suggestion: a lotus meant his birth; a parasol held over a riderless horse was his Renunciation; the Wheel represented him teaching the Dharma; and so forth.

By the first century A.D. commerce with the Greek world had brought about a taste for naturalistic human figures, and under the Indo-Scythian kings, the artists of Mathura and Gandhara first ventured to carve the Master's likeness. Gradually a typical Buddha-image developed, the result of the artists' intuition, as are our conceptions of Christ and Moses.

He was portrayed as having the slightly tilted eyes of a Nepalese and the straight aquiline profile of the Ksha-triya. His lips are finely articulated and usually wear a smile, a curious feature in one who would one day be called a "pessimistic" philosopher. He is slender, but smooth pads of flesh are to be seen on face and body, as if the artists wished to express in this way their sense of the mildness and kindness of his character.

The seemly order of Nirvana expressed in stone. From a votive
relief at Mathura, 5th century A.D. The small curls
"turning upwards and growing to the right" are among the
magical birth-signs of a Great Man. Another is the peculiar
shape of head "like a royal turban."

*Courtesy Government of India Tourist Office*

All these features are brought into harmony by an expression of supernal calm—the seemly order of Nirvana expressed in stone. It is the face of a man who lives in the world and yet out of it.

No doubt Buddha spent much time alone in the wilderness in a state of trance. He liked to be by himself, and he advised everyone to imitate the solitary habits of the rhinoceros. In the legends we often glimpse him pacing back and forth, lost in contemplation; sometimes Ananda is nearby, keeping intruders away.

Nevertheless, the ideas that emerged from these thoughtful interludes were broadcast to the world with the zeal and flair of a politician on campaign. Buddha had "the common touch." He knew how to make people stand still and listen.

People in general called him Sakyamuni—the Sakya Sage; in his old age they said the "Great Recluse." His disciples called him "the Blessed," or "the Enlightened One," and they addressed him as "lord." He referred to himself as "the Truth-finder" and called them simply "monks" except when he was especially pleased with them, when he called them Brahmins. For although he was opposed to the caste system, he admired the ideal Brahmin way of life which called for frugal, modest thoughtfulness. He did not wish to drag the high castes down. He wished everybody to be considered high caste. Once a rude and conceited Brahmin wanted to know what Buddha thought a Brahmin was, and he received the reply, "One who is not conceited."

Buddha did not know that he was starting a new

religion distinct from his own. He believed, as Christ did, that he was rediscovering in his own religion truths that had been forgotten. "I have seen an ancient Path," he said, and he called it the Aryan or Noble Path in honor of his Vedic ancestors.

In view of the religious strife that has shaken our western history, it is surprising to us to find that Buddha did not come into dangerous conflict with the powerful political Brahmins of his day. These members of the highest Hindu caste lived at the courts of kings as wise men, advisers, priests, soothsayers, and experts. A typical encounter between Buddha and court Brahmins took place when Buddha was invited to a meal by King Bimbasara of Rajagriha: "And the Magadha Brahmins and householders respectfully saluted the Blessed One and sat down near him; some exchanged with him greetings and complaisant words; some bent their clasped hands toward him, and some made known their name and family name and sat down near him; and some sat down near him silently."

Yet Buddha was making no secret at all of the way he felt about some of these professional gentlemen. He said that they were "tricksters, droners out of holy words for pay, diviners, exorcists, ever hungering to add gain to gain." And those who lived on offerings at temples and holy wells, he called "tank and shrine Brahmins." As for their sacrificial duties, he was horrified by them. "How can a system which requires the infliction of misery on animals be called a religious system? And how, if one's hands are defiled by blood, can the shedding of more blood restore them to purity?"

We can only assume that many of the Brahmins agreed with Buddha. The skeptical, almost atheistic, and argumentative spirit of the age was protecting him from persecution. His charm of manner, his tactfulness and common sense, his lack of bigotry in any respect, must have mollified possible enemies. "Brahmin, I do not praise every sacrifice; yet I do not withhold praise from every sacrifice. A sacrifice that involves butchery of living creatures, I do not condone. But a long-established charity, or an offering for the welfare of a clan: such a sacrifice should the thoughtful celebrate."

He was bent on ennobling existing customs rather than on destroying them.

Another reason for the absence of conflict with the parent religion was the nature of Hinduism itself. It is not a dogmatic religion with a set of rules that have to be defended. It is "synthetic;" that is, it has the power to embrace and absorb all ideas like a giant Mother-of-thought. That is why so many queer sects and odd religious customs flourish in India: this Mother loves her idiot children as well as her intelligent ones.

This large tolerance had grown out of the original grand conception of God that had been formulated in Aryan times by the Vedic sages: "That which exists is One, though the wise call It by many names." By Buddha's day, Hindu philosophers had built up an explanation of this enormous unity. They called it the World Soul, the Atman, which, they said, permeates all thought and matter. The Atman not only unites man with God, but everything man may think or do. It unites everything that exists. It unites all the gods in the world, the best and the worst of them.

It is impossible to offend this way of thinking. Even atheism does not offend it; for Atman must dwell in the negative as well as in the positive. Atheism, according to the Hindu, is just a way of coming to God by a roundabout route.

Buddha the practical man had all sorts of arguments against Brahministic ritual, and he never ceased to deplore the caste system. But Buddha the sage had even more radical objections regarding this World Soul. He did not deny its existence. But he said it might just as well be ignored, since it did not permeate all thought and matter.

Man stands alone. He is not permeated by Atman. He is not part of a harmonious, united universe. He is totally astray, lost in the desert of eternity. The reason for his plight is his own ignorance.

It is up to man, said Buddha, to conquer his ignorance. Only after that will he be fit to be absorbed back into the perfect purity of the Norm, Nirvana, wherein his individuality is drowned. "When the river reaches the sea, its name-and-shape is lost. We don't speak of a river, we just say the sea."

This was Buddha's view of the meaning of life on earth. It was just the sort of argument the Hindu thinkers loved to get their teeth into. How could they dream of persecuting Buddha? He was, like themselves, engaged in an endless quest of the mind, searching for truth, rejecting error: it was much better to invite him to luncheon and get him into a battle of wits.

"Where exactly is this Nirvana, Venerable Master?" asked the head Brahmin of a village.

"Wherever the Dharma is obeyed," said Buddha.

"Do I understand you correctly? The Nirvana is not a place, and being nowhere it is without reality."

"You do not understand me correctly. Listen and answer: where does the wind dwell?"

"Nowhere."

"Ah, then, there is no such thing as wind."

"I feel the force of your teaching, but I cannot grasp it," said the Brahmin. "Forbear with me again, I pray you: is not reasoning and knowledge the same?"

What is personal identity? What is change? What is sameness? Is there such a thing as self-agency? On down the complex twists and turns of philosophical thought Buddha would wander with the Brahmin sages, and they would lead and dodge each other, and here and there stop to dissect a parable. But courtesy ruled their conduct, and aside from occasional testy outbursts, such as "I have never heard of such a thing!" or "Am I wasting *all* my words?" the dialogues that have survived for us to read are lively with the sheer joy of argument.

Sometimes, no doubt, in that age of controversy Gautama had to deal with those who were more conceited than they were wise, like one Saccaka, a philosopher who announced, "I know no ascetic, no Brahmin, no teacher, no master, no head of a school, even though he calls himself the holy supreme Buddha, who, if he face me in debate, would not totter, tremble, quake, and from whom the sweat would not pour. For if I attacked a lifeless pillar with my language, it would totter, tremble, and quake: how much more a human being?"

Buddha, however, held aloof from futile bickering and wrangling, and he avoided such raging religious ego-maniacs like the plague. He preferred not to answer questions at all than to take sides in an argument he considered pointless.

He was amazingly considerate of other sects. One day, for example, a prominent general, a Jain, decided he would like to become a Buddhist. He was dumfounded when Buddha—who knew that this man's rich family was one of Mahavira's main supporters—urged him to re-consider.

"If any other teacher had converted *me*," exclaimed the general, "he would march up and down the streets carrying banners. But you tell me to reconsider."

"It is proper that a well-known person like yourself should consider carefully every move he makes," said Buddha; and he refused to accept the general as a lay disciple until he promised that if Jain monks should come begging to his door, he would not refuse them alms.

Other sects were not always so kind to Buddha. The story is told that one rival teacher hired a disreputable woman to hover around a place where he was meditating alone, making sure that people noticed her going there. After a few months she accosted him in public.

"You!" she shouted, "You know how to enjoy the

pleasures of love, but what about me and my baby?"

At that moment the piece of wood she had arranged under her sari, to lend force to her words, came loose and thumped on the ground. "There!" laughed Buddha. "There's your baby! Born too soon!"

When in the last century western scholars began to translate and study the teachings of Buddha—whom they sensed to be a person comparable in history only to Christ—he made them perfectly frantic with his perverse no-God, no-prayer, no-priest, no-soul, no-immortality religion in which the Golden Rule shows up as advice to forget others and serve yourself. They had many acrimonious skirmishes with each other, and indeed with their own scholarly consciences, in their desire to spruce him up and make his ideas more pleasing to proper Victorians. One man even refused to believe that such a person as Buddha could ever have abandoned his wife.

Now that the texts (thanks to the efforts of these same gentlemen) have been completely translated into western languages, and eastern beliefs in general are better understood, it is possible to disentangle Buddha from our religious preferences and track him down on his own ground.

Buddha did not believe in prayers either for supplication or for forgiveness of sin, because he thought that the Law of Karma made nonsense of such petitions. Man's fate, he said, is not in the hands of God, it is in his own. It is decided by his own thoughts and actions. "I am the result of my own deeds, heir to deeds, having deeds for matrix, deeds for kin; to me the deeds come home again; whatever deed I do, whether good or evil, I shall become its heir . . . let men, women, and monks contemplate this thought often."

Evil thoughts and deeds can only be expiated by good ones. Good fortune depends on good thoughts and deeds performed in a past life or the present one. Thus, by following the Eightfold Path one automatically brings the fantastic force of the Universe over to one's side. How much safer than prayer! Buddha would have congratulated the poet William E. Henley for his famous lines:

> *I am the master of my fate,*
> *I am the captain of my soul.*

Once this point of view is understood, it is easy to see why Buddha had odd notions about doing good to others. It is obviously sheer vanity to suppose that you can do good or evil to others. You are really doing it to yourself.

Since the moral man has only to do good and let the Law of Karma work for him, priests with their sacrifices are obviously unnecessary, according to Buddha. However, he would have approved of the practice of confession. He said that one who recognizes a sin and confesses it has already entered upon the threshold of the Path.

Even-mindedness is a large word in Buddha's vocabulary —that very quality which is the goal of modern psychiatric techniques. But he would have thought his Eightfold Path a swifter and more practical method of achieving it.

He did not believe in prolonged mulling over one's vile emotions. He believed in kicking them out. The intellect was the instrument for doing this. One can exercise free will in what one thinks and feels as well as in what one does. The human mind is a tower of limitless strength which can *choose* to love instead of to hate; to forgive instead of to harbor malice; to give instead of to take.

"Make what is right become. It is possible to make what is right become. Were it not possible to make what is right become, I would not say, 'Make what is right become.' But because it is possible, therefore I say, 'Make what is right become.' "

This message, affirming man's superiority over his life's conditions, is one of the strengths of Buddhist belief.

Buddha's "atheism" also has to be understood in relation to his own philosophy. Buddha did not deny the existence of the Hindu gods. But his metaphysical ideas compelled him to the conclusion that they were only "caused" beings like ourselves, bound by the same inexorable Law of Karma: if they behaved virtuously they would become perfect and enter Nirvana, and no more would be heard from them; and if they did not behave virtuously they would fall lower and lower in the scale of beings until they lost their place in paradise.

Under this system, a Tibetan legend has it that Mara, the Evil One, eventually became a good Buddhist monk.

Nor can Buddha be called an agnostic in the sense that we use this word—as not knowing if there is a Supreme Deity or not. He simply believed that speculation about this—and much else—was a waste of good mental energy which had better be applied to practicing the moral law. Once some learned Brahmins tackled him on this subject. He said, "Suppose a man is in love with a most beautiful woman and dreams of her day and night. But he does not know whether she is tall or short, or of what caste, or of dark or fair complexion. He does not even know her name. Would you say that the talk of that man about that woman is wise or foolish?"

The Brahmins had to admit that the talk was foolish; and in the end they were made to confess that for all their learning, they knew no more about God than the man knew about the woman.

A monk of Buddha's who had retired into a life of solitary meditation suddenly realized that there were some gaps in his knowledge: "The lord has never explained to me whether the world is eternal or not eternal, finite or infinite, and whether the soul is the same as the body, and whether the Buddha is immortal. This does not suit me at all. I shall go and ask him to explain, and if he does not, I shall leave the Order."

He paid Buddha a visit and put his questions.

"Malunkyaputra," said Buddha, "when you came to the Samgha, did I promise to explain these matters to you?"

"No," admitted Malunkyaputra.

"And anyone who waited for me to do so would die before I did. Malunkyaputra, you are like a man pierced by an arrow, and when his family sends for the surgeon, he says, 'I won't have this arrow pulled out until I know who shot me and whether he was a Kshatriya or a Brahmin; and what his family name is, and where he comes from; and whether he is tall or short, black, dark, yellowish, or what; and what his bow was made of, and whether the bowstring was of hemp, sinew, or fiber, and whether the arrow was feathered with a vulture's wing or a heron's or a peacock's, and whether it was wrapped around with the sinew of an ox or a buffalo or a deer or a monkey'—Malunkyaputra, you'd be dead before you knew all this.

"The religious life does not depend on whether the world is finite or infinite, eternal or not eternal, and whether the soul is the same as the body or whether I am immortal; therefore I have not explained these.

"Suffering have I explained; and the cause of suffering, the destruction of suffering, and the Path that leads to the destruction of suffering. For this is useful, this is concerned with the principle of the religious life.

"Therefore, Malunkyaputra, consider as unexplained what I have not explained; and consider as explained what I have explained."

Is God dead? This modern question would have seemed to Buddha as wasteful as Malunkyaputra's maunderings. He thought of the world as a sort of frantic crazy house with a shuddering floor. He had devised the Eightfold Path as means of walking across it, upright. There was no need to look back or ahead or above. Just keep the Path.

Still, if Buddha had known that he was starting a new religion, one can't help wondering how he would have dealt with mankind's need for a personal God; perhaps he would not be too astonished to find that his followers have made a god out of him.

A legend exists about Buddha when he had become very great and was feeling the loneliness of eminence. He humbly yearned for some person in heaven or on earth to whom he could bow down. He meditated. He cast his mind through the Hindu pantheon, and decided that there was not one god he could reverence; their failings were all too human. As for men, he would not have been the Lord Buddha if there were another sage as worthy of reverence as he.

And so, he was obliged to force his mind, as he had forced the minds of others, away from a personal God to the seemly order of the Norm. "This Norm then, wherein I am supremely enlightened, is the only thing to which I could pay honor and respect."

Entranced by this cold abstract beauty, he ceased to care—at least he told himself that he had ceased to care—whether he was immortal or not.

# 10

# The Lord Buddha:
## THE TEACHER

*Good moral habit is good conscience; good conscience is delight; delight is joy; joy is calm; calm is ease; ease is contemplation; contemplation is knowledge; knowledge is vision; vision is the goal.*

ANGUTTARA-NIKAYA

Buddha spoke in Pali, a derivative of Sanskrit, and, it is believed, the common idiom of Magadha in his time; and probably he spoke also various related dialects understood in the regions where he traveled.

For a good part of the year he was on the road, preaching, exhorting, teaching. Ablaze in his sunlit robe and surrounded by a band of disciples, he traveled across the Ganges Valley and back again, passing through villages and towns, some of which, like Pataliputra—Patna—were to become great in history, and others were to fade from the earth.

Wherever he went he was besieged by the local Brahmins who wanted to engage him in knotty argument, headmen who wanted him to sit down and eat the food they had provided before it got cold, rich people who wanted him to sleep in their grove instead of in somebody else's, ordinary people holding out their hands in the prayerful Indian greeting, and young girls casting flowers beneath his feet.

We imagine him advancing through the crowds, beaming with friendliness, perhaps a little plump from good curries spiritualized upon his tongue, and we suspect that he loved being the greatest Teacher of his time and enjoyed having a fuss made of him.

He would be led to a prepared place under a great shade tree, such as the banyan, which served as the village town hall and auditorium. There he would sit on the clean grass mat the townspeople had made for him, take off all but a couple of the flower garlands that had been thrown around his neck, while the young girls came forward to wash his feet, and those of his monks. Then they were served with food, "both hard and soft"; but they ate from their own begging bowls, according to the rule, so that they would not be tempted into gluttony. When they had done, and had carefully cleaned their bowls, the Lord Buddha would "give thanks" with a discourse, delivered with imagination, love, and urbanity. He had a good voice, "clear and distinct for expounding the meaning."

He took pains with the general public and felt at home with them: "And why? It is these who dwell with me for light, with me for shelter, me for stronghold, me for refuge." He was enchanted to discover among the common folk those who were uncommon. Passing through a certain village, he refused to say one word, but sat in

Buddha among his disciples. A stele of the 6th century, now in the Boston Museum of Fine Arts.

*Courtesy The Bettmann Archive*

silent meditation until a certain weaver's daughter, sixteen years old, whom he knew to be an intelligent and thoughtful child, had finished her daily work and could listen to him. She came and timidly sat down. "Where have you come from, child?" he asked.

"I don't know, reverend sir," she replied.

The people murmured. What a stupid answer! Why hadn't she said outright that she had just come from the weaver's shop?

"Well, why didn't you?" asked the Lord Buddha.

"Because you knew that already. And so I thought you had meant something else: where was I before I was born, or something like that."

For the sake of such people, Buddha would return to the same village again and again.

He had something to say to everyone. He never ceased to exhort businessmen to be honest in their dealings and fastidious in their way of life. "One of wrong moral habit not only fails to amass wealth, but loses it owing to sloth. His evil reputation is spread abroad, and when he is in the company of distinguished people, he finds that he is embarrassed."

To the boys he said, "Certain people are to be reckoned as foes masquerading as friends: the windbag, the smooth talker, and the wastrel.

"The windbag greets you with talk about past deeds; he boasts about future deeds; but when need arises, he points to his own ill luck.

"The smooth talker is always ready for mischievous deeds, but not for good ones. He sings your praises to your face, but behind your back speaks ill.

"The wastrel is your mate in drinking and in roaming the streets at all hours; he is always ready to gamble and to go loafing with you at festivals.

"But all these are foes," said Buddha, "masquerading as friends."

And he said to the girls, "Train yourselves, girls. Whatever husband your parents give to you, for his sake be up early, be the last to retire, order all things sweetly, and speak affectionately. Honor those he honors. When guests come, offer them a seat and water. Be deft and nimble at homecrafts and understand your work thoroughly so as to get it done quickly. Watch over the work of servants. Know the care of the sick. Guard your husband's wealth, corn, silver, and gold, and do not behave as a robber, a thief, or a wastrel in regard to it.

"Then, after you die, you will arise among angels, in lovely form."

And he said, "A house where mother and father are honored is a house of God. For parents were once gods to their young tribe; and once they were teachers. Therefore are they worthy of offerings."

Like all the wandering teachers, he was available for the solving of human dilemma. An aged man once complained to him about his wretched health and asked Buddha to say something to cheer him up.

"True it is, true it is, housefather," said Buddha. "Your body is weak and burdensome. For anyone dragging such a body around, to claim one moment's health would be sheer foolishness.

"Therefore, housefather, teach yourself this: 'Though my body is sick, my mind shall not be sick.' Thus, housefather, teach yourself."

A woman came to him once, holding to her breast her dead son. He had been playing by the river when a snake bit him, and from one minute to the next he was dead. The mother refused to believe it. After trying to revive him, she had gone from one holy man to another, imploring their help; all looked at her with pity and told her to bury her child.

She came to Buddha, asking him to give her son's life back. "That I will, sister," he said, "but you must bring me some medicine. I shall want a seed of black mustard; and you must get it by begging. But remember! You must beg it from a household where there has been no death, of mother or father or wife or husband or child or kin or any loved one."

The mother went off eagerly, begging at many houses before the Master's lesson came home to her: there was not a household anywhere that had not mourned. When she realized that the whole world shared her suffering, it lightened, and she buried her child.

He settled marital arguments, dealt with in-law problems, helped kings and chieftains with their decisions. He did not hesitate to meddle in politics; indeed his equable and fair mind was often in demand by the squabbling tribes, and it is pleasant to watch him appealing to emotions of which he did not approve, in order to gain a good end. Once two clans, about to massacre each other in an argument about a dam they were jointly

building, called him to arbitrate their case. Buddha said
to their kings: "What is the dam made of?"

"Sticks and stones," replied the kings.

"Now tell me—what is of greater value in this world?
Sticks and stones or royal Kshatriya blood?"

"Royal Kshatriya blood!" cried the kings in unison.

"Well, then . . ."

He occupied himself with those who had gone astray;
courtesans and criminals. Near his Jetavana Monastery
there lived a frightening person named Angulimala,
which means "Finger-Necklace." He was in the habit,
whenever he murdered someone, of cutting off a finger
to add to the handsome collection he wore around his
neck.

One day, Buddha went walking near his mountain hide-
away, in spite of the warnings of the local people who
tried to head him off. Angulimala saw him, and ran
swiftly behind him, wanting a finger. But Buddha used
*iddhi*, his magic power, to freeze Angulimala in his tracks,
while he walked calmly on.

The robber, finding himself unable to move his feet,
became terrified, and he cried out, "Stop! Stop!" But
Buddha, moving on, said, "I have stopped, Angulimala.
Now why don't you stop?"

"I am stopped," screeched Angulimala frantically. "I
can't move! You are the one who is moving."

"Oh, no," replied Buddha. "I am still and calm in my
behavior toward all living things. But you are running
about frantically destroying them. Why don't you stop?"

Shortly thereafter, Prasenajit, King of Kosala, called
at Jetavana and spoke of the atrocious Angulimala, whom

he was determined to persecute with goad and sword.

"Suppose there were a robber," said Buddha, "who, having given up his life of crime, ate but one meal a day and followed the Eightfold Path. What would you do?"

"I would do him reverence," replied Prasenajit.

Buddha pointed to a quiet monk: "There is Angulimala."

Prasenajit did him reverence with his hair standing on end.

But it was on his monks of the Samgha that Buddha showered the chief treasures of his heart and mind. They were his thousands of sons, his offspring. He regarded them as the good soil in whom he would plant the Dharma.

Still there were times when Buddha looked at the Samgha and found it wanting. The monks were often unruly; they hooted out of windows, let the rubbish pile up, quarreled and threw dirty water about, got drunk, ran after women, and made up idiotic games to pass the time away.

"Alone, man is as God," Buddha was heard to say, "in twos men dwell as the lesser gods; in threes they are as a village; more than this is a mob."

He saw fit to confide in a horse trainer. "How do you train horses, Kesi?"

"By gentleness and by harshness, lord."

"And if neither of these works?"

"Then I destroy the horse, lord. Otherwise he would ruin my reputation as a trainer. But, lord, you are a matchless teacher of men. How do you train men?"

"By gentleness and by harshness."

"And if a man does not respond to either of these methods?"

"Then I destroy him."

"You! Destroy a man? You would not destroy a fly!"

"When a man is told by me and by other learned monks that he can never put his foot upon the Path—then, Kesi, he is destroyed."

With his teaching of "cool" passions, "cool" detachment, "cool" involvement with the world, it is not surprising that the Lord Buddha found upon his hands some coolly selfish monks. One day he passed by a cell and saw a monk, ill, helpless, and deserted, lying in filth. With Ananda, he washed and tended him and they remade his bed. Then he called a gathering of the Order.

"Monks, is there a monk lying ill in this monastery?"

"Yes, lord."

"And is there no one to wait on him?"

"No, lord."

"And why?"

"He is of no use to us, hence we do not wait on him."

"Monks, you have no mothers or fathers to wait upon you. If you do not wait upon one another, who will wait upon you? Monks, whoever among you would wait upon me, let him wait upon the sick."

Compassion was the emotion that had brought the divine Buddha out of heaven to live on earth; and compassion is the keynote of the teaching of the "historical Buddha."

When one of the monks earnestly strove, Buddha's eye selected him from among the thousands in the Samgha. A young brother called Panthaka was of slow intelligence: he could not learn by heart nor achieve even the first stage of trance. His fellow monks and superiors told him he had better leave the Order. He went and stood by the park gate, hating to leave, and yet not daring to remain.

Buddha was on his way to luncheon with some notables of the town when he became aware of Panthaka's dilemma. He approached the young man, and leading him by the arm, took him to a quiet place in the park where he gave him the spotlessly clean napkin he used for wiping his feet. "Here—meditate upon this clean thing," he said, "and do not let your mind wander from it for an instant."

Panthaka sat and stared at the napkin, exerting all his will. Time passed. His consciousness contracted, and he fell into a light trance. Suddenly he became aware that someone was standing next to him. It was a messenger from Buddha, calling him to lunch. When he arrived, Buddha made him sit down next to him and signaled for the serving to begin. He had refused to touch food before Panthaka achieved his trance.

Buddha placed mighty emphasis in his preaching to laymen and monks alike on the necessity of individual effort. Among his most famous words are, "I do but point the way: it is for you to sweat and strain."

One of the main points of distinction between the Samgha and the Christian monastic societies is that the Samgha demanded no vow of obedience to the organization as such. Rules of community life were laid down which the monks were expected to obey. But essentially, the Samgha was meant as a refuge for the individual, a place where a man might cultivate his mind intensively, free of everyday distractions, including even rules.

He was given the good advice of older monks and that of the Master himself while he lived, but his was the mind, and his the effort. "Do not be guided by anything told to you," said Buddha, "neither by tradition or recitation, nor logic, nor inference, nor reason, nor Doctrine, even if your teacher tells it. *Know for yourself:* this is right and this is wrong."

He was delighted when people began to think for themselves. A monk who sat and meditated while his brothers were busy sewing robes was not to be criticized. A small boy Sariputra had under his wing who escaped from his duties in order to follow a train of thought was not to be scolded. Anybody who wished might wander off into the solitudes if he thought he could think better there.

All the same, when the monks thought for themselves and thought wrong, Buddha was not the man to gloss over it. One group, cooped up together during the rainy season, thought they would better avoid quarreling and Wrong Speech if they took a vow of silence for the duration. When Buddha heard of this, he exclaimed, "Indeed! What do they think they are, keeping silence? A herd of cattle? A herd of rams? Or are they just lazy? This won't do. How is anyone going to hear the Truth if monks keep silence?"

It was much better to quarrel, he said, and then after the rains were over stand up before the elders, admit the fault, and accept penance. Penance was not in the shape of self-punishment. It was in the shape of positive action, something that would count in the monk's Karma. "It is not the custom of the Truth-finder to exact 'Penalty, penalty!' It is the custom of the Truth-finder to exact 'Deeds, deeds!' "

Whether a monk was struggling with the first stages of the Path, or whether he was seeking the transcendent experience of the trance, he had a terrible time detaching himself from Self. On many different occasions and in many different words, Buddha pounded home his central Doctrine: that everything one could think of or conceive, including the component parts of the Self, was in a constant state of motion and change. The one quiet thing was the Norm, and in order to get to it, one had to throw Self to the winds.

In order to help them despise that most obvious component of the Self, the body, he told them things about it that would have outraged the Greek philosophers, who admired the human form. Taken inch by inch, inside and out, what was the body? A bag of samples, with horrid holes here and there. And what oozed from the holes? Eye-excrement, ear-excrement, nose-excrement, and so on. "And when the body is dead, swollen and livid, who cares for it? Dogs, jackals, worms, crows, vultures."

He bade them sit in the graveyard and contemplate the carrion-gnawed corpses there, splattered with blood, held together by disgusting tendons; and then they were to reflect that their own bodies were also nothing more or less than gruesome chains of bones.

He filled his discourses with parables, picturesque and always to the point. He was witty and delighted in paradoxes and puns. Sometimes he delivered a teaching that could be understood in two different ways, to give his monks a subject of debate, humorous or profound.

From the dialogues that have been preserved one has a sense of his infinite patience and consideration for his pupils. His tone is assertive, but not didactic. He persuaded rather than commanded. "I exhort you, I protest to you . . ." Even in expressing abstruse ideas, he always asked his monks questions he knew they could answer, so that he could then reply approvingly, "Quite so," or "Well said!" before going on to the next step. He did not so much lead them as walk side by side with them, merely choosing the path. He never tangled them up in a maze of riddles or stunned them with his own brilliance or made them look foolish.

Whenever Buddha said something particularly useful, his words were used by the monks for thoughtful meditation. They reflected on them when they went traveling, or while they were begging, with their eyes fixed but a plow's distance ahead of them.

"The victor breeds enmity; the conquered sleeps in sorrow. Regardless of victory or defeat, the calm man dwells in peace."

"A monk who is fond of disputes is walled in by ignorance and understands neither religion nor Gautama's Law."

"Consort with the wise. Follow in the wake of the learned and prudent, as the moon follows the path of the stars."

But it was not altogether by sage advice that the Lord Buddha held his sons close to himself. Often when they gathered around him asking for explanations and opinions, he would reply, "It is not the first time this has happened."

And then a long story would unwind, full of humor, romance, and thrills, all purporting to be his memories of his past lives and all ending happily ever after because someone had behaved virtuously. Once he had been a Monkey with Right Effort; or a Rabbit with Right Views; or a Noble Elephant; or a poor man who prayed to be reborn as a Serpent King and lived to learn his folly.

He used the colors and the manifold threads of his country's folklore to weave for them a vast, crowded tapestry in honor of the Eightfold Path. Five hundred and fifty of these tales survive in a book called the *Jataka*. They are the fairy tales of Buddhist children to this day, and the most complete body of ancient folklore in the world.

All that he said was faithfully learned by heart by his hearers. They did not have to depend on mere good memory. Their powers of recall were trained and developed from the moment they entered the monastery. The form of the legends, in which almost every key episode or significant chain of thought is repeated at least three times, was perhaps devised to make sure that everything was learned with exactitude, not only for the monks' own sakes, but because it was their duty to impress the Buddha's teachings accurately upon others.

And that is why we may still hear the voice of the Lord Buddha pouring forth the timeless thoughts of one who was wise and kind; and we reflect with amazement that though he spoke at the beginning of recorded history, his were among the grandest utterances that were ever to fall from the lips of a man. As when he said, "No scent of flower is borne against the wind, though it were sandal, or incense, or jasmine; but the fragrance of the holy is borne against the wind. Right pervades."

And when he said to you and me: "May all beings be happy and at their ease! May they be joyous and live in safety! All beings, whether weak or strong, omitting none —in high, middle, or low realms of existence, small or great, visible or invisible, near or far away, born or yet to be born—may all beings be happy and at their ease!"

And when he spoke to our generation: "Listen, and I shall explain to you the exact distinctions between living beings. Their origins are various.

"Know you that even among palms and other trees there are marks of distinction according to their family.

"Worms, grasshoppers, even the tiniest ants, are distinctly marked according to their family.

"Know ye that four-footed animals, small and great, and long-backed animals which glide on their bellies and creep on their breasts, are distinctly marked according to their family.

"And again, fish that live in the water and birds which move in the sky are distinctly marked according to their family.

"And in all these kinds of living things, their distinctions are evident from birth.

"But in man there are no such distinct marks: all men have hair, head, ears, eyes, mouth, nose, lips, brows; all have neck, shoulders, belly, back, breast; all have hands, feet, palm, fingernails.

"Among men, distinctions are man-made."

# 11

# *Ill Winds*

*Now there was a certain Noble Elephant, much worried by a crowd of male and female elephants. He had to feed on blades of grass with their tips broken, and they ate the young branches he himself had pulled down.*

UDANA

Thousands of people had only to listen briefly to Buddha expounding the Dharma in order to attain the highest vision, Aharat-ship, sainthood: so the writers of the Buddha-legend want us to believe. They are perhaps contradicted by the Lord Buddha himself who said, "I, monks, do not say that attainment of profound knowledge comes straightaway; nevertheless it does come by gradual training, a gradual doing of what is to be done."

It is rather curious that the tall-tale-tellers deny sainthood to the monk whom generations of Buddhists have loved best after Buddha, his friend and personal attendant, Ananda. Wherever this gentle person went he saw Aharats to the left and right of him, and perfect strangers were forever attaining Aharat-ship before his eyes; but he himself was not an Aharat.

The reason Ananda could not become a Buddhist saint was that he had a flaw: he was not detached from common everyday tenderhearted love. He loved Buddha, lived and breathed for him, thought of nothing but good deeds to perform for his sake. It was he who staved off the crowds who followed the sage about, found him quiet places to have his meal, kept away monks who wanted to plague him, winnowed bad news before it got to his ears. When there was nothing else to do and Buddha was pacing to and fro in meditation, Ananda was as his shadow, one pace behind.

Not until after Buddha died was Ananda able to concentrate on becoming a saint; and until the day he himself died, it was the custom among the monks to blame Ananda for everything that went wrong in the Samgha.

Possibly the greatest blunder for which he had to bear the reproaches of his brethren developed after the death of Suddhodana. Buddha, upon receiving word that his father was seriously ill, hurried to his side and guided him safely into the state of Nirvana. Afterward, he carried out the cremation ceremony according to Hindu custom.

He lingered for a while at the Nigrodha park in order to settle a difference of opinion that had arisen between the Sakyas and the Koliyas about irrigation rights on the river Rohini which divided their lands. One morning he received a sorrowful visitor. It was the widowed Prajapati, his foster mother. She bowed low to him and asked a boon: might she enter the Samgha?

Buddha said No.

Prajapati made this request three times. Everyone she loved was in the Samgha. Her son Nanda was there and

Buddha himself; and soon Rahula would be fully ordained. Three times she was refused, and finally she retired, bowing, with tears streaming down her face.

Buddha left the Nigrodha Grove and traveled to his Pinnacled Tower Monastery at Vaisali, the capital of the Vajji tribe. If he had turned his clairvoyant eye backward, he would have seen Prajapati busily sewing rags together in the company of a number of women. When they had finished making monkish robes, they dyed them yellow, put them on, and followed Buddha to the Pinnacled Tower. There, covered with dust and with swollen feet, they stood on his porch and cried.

Ananda saw them there and asked the reason. Prajapati replied, "Because the lord, the Blessed One, does not allow women to renounce their homes and enter the homeless state under his Doctrine and discipline."

Ananda, always soft-hearted and regardless of Self, entered Buddha's room and sat down beside him. "Prajapati is outside with swollen feet, covered with dust, sorrowful, sad and weeping. She says you won't let women enter the Order. It would be well, lord, if she were permitted to do as she desires."

"Enough, Ananda," said the Lord Buddha.

Ananda persisted; and so did Buddha, earnestly advising Ananda to change his mind on the subject. Instead, Ananda changed his ground: "Lord, tell me this. Are women capable of realizing the grace of conversion? Can they understand the stages of the Path? Can they attain Aharat-ship?"

Caught in the net of his own inexorable logic which maintains that nothing one can see or sense—including sex—is the essential Self, Buddha replied, "They are capable, Ananda."

"Then, lord, if they are capable, and since Prajapati was your aunt and nurse, nourished you and gave you milk —would it not be well if women might be permitted to enter the Samgha?"

Buddha pondered and thought he saw a way out. "Well then, Ananda, if Prajapati wishes to take this step, let her reflect on the following conditions to be revered, reverenced, honored, and never to be transgressed as long as life shall last. In the first place, a nun must always rise up and bow down before a monk and serve him, even if he is only just initiated. She is not to dodge her duties during the rains by living with other nuns at some distant spot where monks cannot keep their eye on them. She is to attend Council meetings without fail, so that if the monks wish to find fault with her they may do so and impose disciplinary measures; but she must never find fault with a monk."

Under these stern conditions Buddha promised he would permit women to enter the Order.

Ananda went out onto the porch and repeated his terms to Prajapati. She did not hesitate a minute. "Tell the lord," she said, "that just as when I was young I used to gather lotus and jasmine to make garlands for my head, so do I take upon me these rules."

Ananda went back into the house and gave the message to his Master who was not at all charmed by it. Buddha liked women, and he was afterward to show patient effort in the instruction of Prajapati. But now he was tasting defeat and he did not enjoy it. "Women are a mildew on a field of rice!" he exclaimed. "They are a blight on sugar cane. If, Ananda, I hadn't given permission for women to enter the Order, the Good Law would have lasted long, for a thousand years. But now that I have given permission, it will last for only five hundred.

"Just as a man builds a dam, Ananda, so that the water shall not overpass, so have I made those rules against the nuns!"

He was both right and wrong. The Good Law has endured much longer than his most optimistic thought; but in countries such as Tibet where the feminine Samgha survived, overpassing has sometimes taken place.

In Buddha's time there was some overpassing too, but on the whole the nuns seem to have behaved themselves; and there were learned and distinguished ones among them. Some accounts state that Buddha's wife, Yasodhara, eventually became a nun.

If there was an elite class of saints in the Samgha, it followed that there was a much larger class of unsaintly persons. Buddha testily wished they wouldn't bother him with squabbles. "Even a teacher who sets store on material things—why even he is not met by higgling and haggling and talk about what his followers will or will not do—so what has all this got to do with me, who live apart from material things?"

Once a monk who was required to rise before the Council and admit a certain fault refused to admit it. He saw no reason why he was at fault. On Buddhist principles, an action is not wrong unless the offender consciously intends a wrongdoing. The monk was nevertheless excommunicated, and on this matter of principle, great dissension arose.

Buddha tried to smooth things over by relating a series of historical crimes, all of which had been resolved by forgiveness on the one hand and admission of guilt on the other. "Do not look long, do not look short. Not by hatred are hatreds calmed. By non-hatred are hatreds calmed."

But he only provoked higher feelings. In the end he got tired of it all. He went off by himself into the forest where he spent three months in deep meditation. One day there came to the grove a lone elephant which, finding it occupied by a holy man, did not harm him, but on the contrary brought him water in its trunk and took up quiet residence nearby. Buddha thought that he achieved silent communion with the beast; that somehow the elephant made him aware that it too was dissatisfied with the rackety herd and that it had sought this place of solitude in order to regain tranquillity of spirit.

After three months the monks, their passions calmed, sought him out and asked forgiveness, which Buddha gladly gave, together with an account of his adventure with the Noble Elephant.

Nanda gave him trouble. This youth, it will be recalled, was Buddha's much younger half brother, and Buddha had somewhat incautiously stolen him away from his bride on his wedding day, using Nanda's exquisite manners as a tool against him. Buddha lived to regret it. Nanda could not keep his beautiful bride out of his mind. Once he tried to run away from the monastery and was hav-

ing some difficulty in closing the gates when Buddha suddenly came along the path. Nanda hid behind a tree, but Buddha saw him. He did not reprimand him, but let him go home to his wife.

But once at home and enjoying the married state, Nanda could not forget Buddha or cease to sing his praises. His wife became so exasperated that she scratched him and drove him away. Back in the monastery, Nanda began to think and chatter about his wife. And so on, back and forth. He was not a good husband, and he was far from a good monk.

Buddha finally settled the matter by magic. One day as Nanda was moaning about how much he missed home, he made the young man see a vision of nymphs in paradise, all far more beautiful than his wife. Thereafter Nanda settled down in the monastery. But whenever his comrades caught him looking particularly holy, they used to ask him which nymph he was going to marry when he got to paradise.

By far the worst wind that ever blew on Buddha came in his old age, from the direction of his cousin Devadatta.

Devadatta, so the legend goes, had been Buddha's rival from early youth. He is presented as a person of many gifts, but his intelligence was worldly and his accomplishments lacked moral foundation.

Still, when he entered the Samgha at about the age of thirty-nine, he seems to have spent the following thirty-three years peacefully at work on Right Concentration, and to have impressed everyone with his earnestness. Sariputra had him proclaimed throughout the town of Rajagriha as a wise and holy monk. Devadatta did not achieve Aharat-ship, though; instead he stopped short with *iddhi,* magical and psychic powers.

*Iddhi* is certainly one of the most fascinating of the mental accomplishments that are said to accompany the methodical practice of deep trance. It includes those possible hidden faculties of the mind which we group under the term ESP, extrasensory perception. The thinker becomes clairvoyant and clairaudient: he is able to see and hear things happening far off and in the future. He can read people's minds. He is a teleportist, able to transport himself and other objects through the air by mental force.

In addition, he can pass through walls, walk on water, change his shape, and cause realistic hallucinations to arise before the eyes of any number of people.

Buddha used *iddhi* on occasion: he had acquired one of his most valuable disciples, Kasyapa, by this means, and had gathered in Angulimala from his life of crime. Once he made a mango tree spring up from the ground bearing real fruit, exactly as Indian magicians do—in one way or another—in modern times. And he had a famous trick, called the Miracle of the Pairs, which must have been a stunning spectacle: he would leap into the air and hang there with fire coming out of the upper part of his body, and water spraying from the lower part; and then in reverse; next with fire from the left side and water from the right; and so on, like a giant Catherine wheel.

Sometimes he shot out duplicate images of himself in all directions, standing, sitting, lying down. This miracle has always been a favorite subject of temple-sculptors, who love to carve Buddhas and Buddhas.

However, Buddha discouraged the use of *iddhi* in the

A Tibetan painting on cotton or jute showing Buddha
surrounded by small replicas of himself. This is a favorite
decorative motif of Buddhist painters and sculptors and
probably derives from one of Buddha's favorite miracles.
*Courtesy The Metropolitan Museum of Art*

Samgha, realizing its dangers. A monk might use it for idle display, or gain; worse still, to obtain power over simple minds. He therefore forbade the display of magical powers, except in unusual circumstances. They were to be treated as a by-product of the trance exercise, not as an end.

This command was later disobeyed in Tibet where the Tantric Sect is rumored to have developed psychic powers to an amazing degree; but it has been obeyed in the southern Buddhist countries which follow the early teachings, and where any monk who finds he can do tricks keeps them to himself.

Devadatta, says the legend, used *iddhi* for personal advantage. First, he assumed the form of a child clothed in a girdle of snakes, and suddenly appeared on the lap of Prince Ajatasatru, King Bimbasara's son and heir, who was terrified.

"Are you afraid of me, O prince?" asked Devadatta.

"Yes," said the prince. "Who are you?"

"I am Devadatta."

"Then be so kind, sir, as to resume the shape of the worthy Devadatta."

Devadatta resumed his own shape, bowl and all, well pleased to see the impression he had made. For a long time afterward he enjoyed the prince's bounty. Every morning and evening Ajatasatru used to visit him accompanied by slaves bearing food consisting of five hundred different dishes with which to regale Devadatta and those monks who were his friends and followers.

In time Devadatta became conceited. "It is I who ought to lead the Samgha instead of my cousin," he

mused. As the awful thought took shape, the power of
*iddhi* left him. He did not mention his loss to anyone;
but Buddha knew, and he pointed Devadatta out, saying,
"That monk has evil wishes which will shortly be re-
vealed."

One day as Devadatta sat with other monks surround-
ing Buddha, he rose from his seat, adjusted his robe, and
courteously approached the Master with his hands
clasped in front of him. "The Blessed One has grown
old, lord," he said. "He is stricken in years and his long
journey is almost run. Why should not the Blessed One
now retire, live at his ease in the enjoyment of hard-
earned happiness? I will be the leader of the Samgha."

Yes, Buddha was old. He was seventy-two. But then,
so was Devadatta. The Master tried to silence his cousin,
but when Devadatta persisted, he burst out with an old
man's exasperation, "I would not give up the Samgha to
Sariputra or Mogallana, still less to you, vile spittle-drib-
bler!"

Devadatta managed to get back to his place with dignity, but he was furious, and malice smoldered in his
heart. Buddha commanded Sariputra, "Send out monks
into the streets of Rajagriha and proclaim against
Devadatta. Let it be known that he was once a good
monk but is so no longer, and that whatever he says or
does is not in accordance with the Doctrine or the
Samgha." This was done.

Having no further powers of his own, Devadatta now
set himself to corrupt Ajatasatru. "Alas, prince, people
do not live as long these days as they used to do. The
chances are that you will not live long enough to become

king. Why not kill your father and become king now?
And I'll kill Gautama and become the Buddha."

Prince Ajatasatru pondered. "This worthy Devadatta
has great insight," he thought, "and he knows what he is
talking about. He is probably giving me good advice."
By nightfall he had worked himself into a rage against
his aged father, and fastening a dagger to his thigh, he
burst into the king's apartments. But his excited behavior
attracted the attention of some ministers who seized and
searched him. The dagger was found.

"What were you going to do, O prince?"

"I wanted to kill the king."

"Who incited you to such a deed?"

"The worthy Devadatta."

Some ministers thought that the worthy Devadatta
ought to have his head chopped off, together with the
entire Samgha, including Buddha. But calmer councils
prevailed and the matter was taken before Bimbasara.
The king spoke to Ajatasatru: "Why did you want to kill
me, my son?"

"Because I wanted the kingdom."

"Ah, you want the kingdom? Then take it!" And
Bimbasara, a faithful follower of the Path, abdicated,
leaving all his troubles in the lap of Ajatasatru.

This happy turn of events served to confirm the new
king's opinion that Devadatta knew exactly what he was
talking about. He showered honors on him and gave him
a troop of men with which to assassinate Buddha.

Buddha was at that time visiting another town, but
Devadatta knew the path by which he would return, and
he stationed a man upon it with orders to kill the Master

on sight. A little farther on he stationed two men with the same directions; farther on, four men; and so on up to sixteen. All were armed with swords, shields, bows, arrows.

The outcome was as you might expect. The assassins, upon sight of the Buddha, were moved to listen to him; once they had listened to him they became Aharats. Buddha walked into Rajagriha accompanied by thirty-one saints.

One of them, however, had the presence of mind to report the fiasco to Devadatta, who responded with surprising good temper. "Never mind, friend, I'll kill the Blessed One myself."

Thereafter for a long time, Devadatta occupied himself with plots against Buddha's life. He crept up a cliff and dislodged a huge stone which hurtled down upon the sage; but the stone caught in a cleft, and only a splinter harmed the foot of Buddha. When Devadatta heard that one of the elephants in the royal stables had become a rogue, he bribed the mahouts to let it loose in Buddha's path when he came begging in the city. The elephant charged down the street with its trunk curled like a snake, emitting fearsome noises, and the crowds scattered right and left and climbed to the housetops where they huddled to watch the awesome sight. "Now elephant will wage war on elephant," they said.

Buddha caused his love to flow out toward the excited animal and the elephant put down its trunk, walked soberly to the place where Buddha was, and stood still to be stroked. "Be thou not mad, O elephant," said Buddha, stroking its forehead, "and do not be careless either, for the careless cannot enter Nirvana."

The elephant retired from the scene bowing backward as if it were in a circus.

Up to this point, Devadatta's record looks black indeed; it also looks fairly unconvincing. We suspect that the ancient chronicler, by piling up the crimes of this large meal-eater and assassin, wishes to throw dust in our eyes so that we will gloss over some sober facts: that for no less than thirty-three years Devadatta had been a good monk, and that he had a following of other monks.

But the chronicler is honest, and now he must bend his pen to his duty, which is to record a historic event, unthinkable as it seemed to him, that in the lifetime of the Lord Buddha there was a schism in the Order. Some monks were discontented with Buddha's leadership of the Samgha.

It may be that at the bottom of the trouble was Buddha's habit in the latter years of his life of spending his retreats at Sravasti. The schism occurred at Rajagriha, where the monks, perhaps feeling neglected, began to find fault, and naturally gravitated toward a leader who felt as they did—and it was Devadatta.

Their main complaint against Gautama was that mild streak we have noted again and again in his character which prompted him to relax, in a number of ways, the stringent rules he had originally imposed upon the Samgha.

In trying to discern what are likely to be the actual events, Devadatta changes shape before our eyes. Instead of a satanic juggler, we see an ascetic with a stern look, a sort of Hebrew prophet who foresees the doom of the Order if Buddha's tolerant attitudes are allowed to prevail. No doubt Devadatta was a tactless man. When he went begging in Rajagriha he used to take a regiment of followers, all holding out their bowls, much to the indignation of householders. When this came to Buddha's ears, he made a new rule: "No more than three monks shall enjoy alms from the same house: this to prevent mischievous monks from showing they have support; and out of compassion for the laity."

Probably Devadatta was sincerely convinced that Buddha was getting a little senile, and he therefore tried to persuade Buddha to abdicate. Snubbed for his pains, he retired. But shortly afterward, he again appeared before Buddha, this time with a party of his followers, and they laid before the Master, in politest terms, what we may take to be the historical facts behind this first serious schism in the Samgha.

"Lord," said Devadatta, "you have many times declared the advantages of a man who wishes for little of the world's goods and who has quelled his passions and is full of faith and zeal for the Doctrine.

"In our opinion, lord, the following five things are desirable for anyone wishing to achieve this state of mind:

"Monks ought not to live in monasteries, but in the woods.

"Monks should be required to beg their meals always, and not be permitted to accept invitations to eat at private houses.

"Monks should clothe themselves in cast-off rags, and not accept gifts of robes from laymen.

"Monks should dwell all their lives under trees, and never sleep under a roof.

"Monks ought to abstain from eating fish or flesh."

These were the simple requests of Devadatta. Aside from his vegetarian preferences, he only wished to return to Buddha's original rules. We may imagine Buddha, aware of this, fidgeting with his robes and carefully considering his answer. He had spent his life pointing to a Middle Path along which as many people as possible could travel. He was not against asceticism for those it suited, but it is possible only to a few. Nevertheless he knew that the general public and many monks also tended to agree with Devadatta: at the heart of Hinduism lies the conviction that asceticism and holiness dwell together.

It was a crisis, and Buddha knew it. But for all his easygoing ways, he was never in two minds about anything.

"No, Devadatta. My views are clear. Whoever wishes to do so may dwell in the woods, and whoever wishes to do so may dwell in a monastery. Whoever wishes to do so may beg for alms, and whoever wishes to do so may accept invitations from the laity. Whoever wishes to do so may wear rags, and whoever wishes to do so may accept a gift of robes from laymen. Sleeping under trees, Devadatta, has always been allowed by me for eight months of the year.

"As for the eating of fish or flesh, the points are clear: any monk may eat it, provided that he has not seen or heard or suspected that a living thing has been caught and killed especially to provide him with a meal."

Dismissed, Devadatta and his followers left the Order,

and thereafter they lived as they chose. Their sect survived for several centuries.

Buddha said Devadatta was bound for hell; he then made up for such Wrong Speech by predicting that in the course of many improving lives, Devadatta would at last become a good monk and an Aharat. Nevertheless his original hasty remarks became known, and Mahavira, leader of the Jains, thought he saw a way to trap Buddha. He persuaded a young prince, a follower of his, to win fame by asking Gautama a question he would not be able to answer. "Ask him if he ever says anything unpleasant or disagreeable to others. If he says Yes, ask him how he differs from the common people who are also prone to say disagreeable things. If he says No, ask him why he said that Devadatta was going to hell, which I happen to know made Devadatta exceedingly angry."

The prince invited Buddha to luncheon and put the question: did Buddha ever utter words disagreeable to others?

"Sometimes," said Buddha. Indicating a baby on the prince's lap, he asked him if he would hesitate to save the child's life at the risk of hurting him a little.

"Speech that I know to be untrue, useless, and disagreeable to others, I do not speak. Speech that I know to be true, but useless and also disagreeable to others, I do not speak. Speech that I know to be true and useful, and yet disagreeable to others—in that case I know the right time to say it. And speech that is true, useful, agreeable, and timely, that I speak."

# 12

# The Great Decease

*Now art thou seen, O Builder! Nevermore shalt thou
build the house. Thy beams are broken, cast down is
thy cornerstone. My mind is set upon Nirvana.*

DHAMMAPADA

Buddha lived to see his tribe wiped out by the Kosalas.
It came about in this way.

Prasenajit, king of Kosala, a friend of Buddha's, thinking to pay him a compliment and at the same time wind
up his long quarrel with the Sakyas, asked for a Sakya
maiden as a bride. The Sakyas, out of sheer spite, hood-
winked him into marrying a girl who was the daughter of a
Sakya noble and a slave woman. Years later, when her son
had grown and sat on the throne, he learned of his low-
caste blood and was outraged. He led his Kosalans against
the Sakyans and killed them—men, women, babes, suck-
lings; and he put their nobles to torture. A few escaped.

Buddha was eighty. Death stalked around him. Sariputra, who was seriously ailing, visited him one day and
uttered with unaccustomed emotion: "Lord, such faith
do I have in thee that I think there never was, nor is,
nor ever will be any Teacher who is a greater and wiser

Enlightened One than you." Buddha got him to confess that, after all, he could not read the minds of Enlightened Ones past or future, still less the one who was sitting next to him. But it had been good to hear such words from Sariputra.

It was their last interview. Sariputra, having lived a houseless life, took a notion to die in the room where he was born. He wished also to convert to the Dharma his mother, a stubborn old Brahmin lady. He left for home, made a Buddhist of his mother, and then died in his bed. Upali, the former barber, fell heir to his position as Buddha's "general."

A fortnight later, Sariputra's friend Mogallana was meditating alone on a hillside above Rajagriha when he was set upon by robbers. Though he possessed nothing they could want, they broke his bones and left him to die.

"Truly, this company of mine seems empty," said Buddha.

Ajatasatru had finally managed to kill peaceful old King Bimbasara, and he was eager to begin laying the foundation of an empire which would, in time, unite the whole of northern India and, under the Maurya kings, become the first Indian empire. He intended to begin by falling upon the Vajjis, his northerly neighbors on the other side of the Ganges, and bring them to disaster and ruin. It occurred to him to send his prime minister to tell Buddha about this plan in the hope of surprising the sage into making a prophecy about it.

Buddha received the prime minister in a cave on the "Vulture's Peak," the highest of the five mountains that shelter Rajagriha. After hearing the king's purpose, he merely said that some time ago he had prophesied to the Vajjis that as long as they did not neglect public meetings or quarrel among themselves, esteemed their elders, and refrained from kidnaping the girls of other clans—that long might they expect to live in peace. "Have you heard, Ananda, that the Vajjis are behaving themselves in this way?" he inquired.

"Lord, so I have heard," replied Ananda.

"We may take it then," said the prime minister briskly, "that this undertaking will not prosper at this time, and that some diplomatic measures will be needed in order to cause dissension among the Vajjis."

The record of Buddha's last year of life does not explain why, directly after his conversation with the prime minister, he chose to travel straight into the eye of trouble, the land of the Vajjis. Perhaps he wished to warn them. Perhaps he felt the need to go northward toward the Himalayan regions where he was born. He traveled with Ananda and other old friends by easy stages, stopping frequently to deliver addresses. They reached a small town on the Ganges called Pataligama.

This town—which we know as Patna—was to become in the near future the capital of the Maurya Empire, Pataliputra. It was already flourishing: fortresses were being built in preparation for the Vajji war. A crowd of citizens welcomed Buddha and led him to their resthouse where, after his feet had been washed, he settled himself against a pillar and lectured them about honesty in business dealings. They informed him that they were going to name a city gate after him, and also the main ford over the Ganges. He is said to have predicted then the future greatness of their city. However, he did not have the energy to cross Gautama Ford. Instead he used *iddhi* to whisk himself across to the further bank where he sat down and waited for his monks to flounder through the shallows.

He was tired. He had a spell of depression; he even wondered if he was really an Enlightened One. Perhaps he and these old friends who had faith in him did not understand the Four Noble Truths as well as they thought they did, and that was why they were condemned to stagger across rivers in their old age.

The news at Nadika in the Vajji territory was gloomy. There had been an epidemic of deaths and several monks and devout nuns had gone their way, as had a large number of valued lay disciples. Ananda began to plague Buddha with questions: where had they gone? what were they doing? would they be born again? Buddha obliged him with detailed information, but finally balked. "There is nothing strange, Ananda, that a human being should die. But that as each one does, you should come to me with these inquiries is certainly tedious."

They arrived at Vaisali, the Vajji capital, and Buddha took up residence in a beautiful grove belonging to a courtesan named Ambapali, which means "Row of Mangoes." She was tremendously flattered, and came in her carriage to pay him reverence. Alighting at the edge of the grove, she wended through the trees and took a respectful seat to one side of Buddha. He began to talk to her to very good effect: she was instructed, aroused, and gladdened by his words. She invited him, with his following, to take his meal at her house on the following day. Buddha expressed his assent by silence, as was the custom.

As Ambapali rolled away from the grove, there was quite a traffic jam when her carriage tangled with a fleet of grand state carriages full of Vajji nobles, the chief men of Vaisali, who had heard of Buddha's arrival. They had come to invite him to lunch on the following day and they had gone to some pains to make themselves attractive. The dark-skinned ones had dressed in dark clothes and ornaments, the pale-skinned ones had put on pale clothes and ornaments, and the ruddy ones were in red clothes and ornaments. As their carriages drove up against that of Ambapali, axle to axle, yoke to yoke, they asked her what she was doing visiting a holy man, and she said that she had invited Buddha to lunch.

"Give up this meal, Ambapali, for a hundred thousand gold pieces!" cried the Vajjis.

"Not for all Vaisali!" she replied and crashed through their lines. Glumly they left their carriages and entered the grove. "Behold!" exclaimed Buddha as they burst upon his sight. "Let those monks who have never seen angels in heaven gaze upon this company of Vajjis. And let those who have compare them!"

But the Vajjis were in no mood for witticisms. They said, "May the Exalted One do us the honor of taking his meal with us tomorrow?"

"I have already promised to go tomorrow to the mansion of Ambapali the courtesan."

The Vajjis cast up their hands in exasperation saying, "We are outdone by this Mango-girl, we are outwitted by this Mango-girl." Buddha's discourse failed to gladden them and they departed in sore spirits.

The next day the company ate sweet rice and cakes at Ambapali's mansion. When she had done serving them, she sat down on a low stool beside Buddha, and said, "Lord, I present my grove to the Samgha." And Buddha thanked her.

It was June and the rainy season was about to begin. There was no shelter at Ambapali's grove, and besides, Buddha felt the need of a quiet retreat. He told his monks to find shelter where they wished in Vaisali while he went alone, except for Ananda, to a quiet suburb, where they settled themselves, apparently in an empty house, while the rains came thundering down.

One day Buddha was taken violently ill with stomach pains, and for a while he lay near death. He told himself, "I cannot pass away without taking leave of the disciples. I must exert my will to bend this sickness down and keep my hold on life."

He exerted his disciplined will and the sickness abated. In time he recovered sufficiently to sit with Ananda on the porch. Ananda said, "When I saw you suffering, my body became weak as a creeper and the horizon grew dim. And yet I knew you would not let yourself go without leaving instructions for the Order."

"What instructions, Ananda?" asked Buddha gently. "I have no instructions for the Order. All my life I have taught the Dharma and have kept no closed fist on it. When I am gone, someone else will think he ought to lead the Samgha, and it is for him to give instructions.

"I am old, Ananda, and full of years. My journey is drawing to its close. I have reached my sum of days, I am in years eighty and more. And just as a worn-out cart, Ananda, can be kept going only with the help of thongs, so my body can be kept going only by bandaging it up.

"Be ye lamps unto yourselves, Ananda. Be ye a refuge to yourselves. Hold fast to the Dharma as a lamp. Hold fast as a refuge to the Dharma. Look not for refuge to anyone besides yourselves.

"And those who look to themselves, Ananda, now or when I am dead, they among my monks will reach the higher wisdom."

By the time the season of rains had drawn to its close in September, Buddha was on his feet again and well enough to go begging in Vaisali. But he was not content. Doubts were at him again. We can only conjecture their nature. He had spent his lifetime gazing with adoration upon this beautiful abstraction, this mathematical Norm, this "solitude that is so hard to love—Nirvana." Now that he was about to meet it, could he have feared it? The Great Recluse had given himself so largely to the world that in his own time, as in ours, he was larger than life, and he knew it. Perhaps it was hard for him to think of being a mere "dewdrop slipping into the shining sea."

One day he said, "Ananda! Take up the mats. We'll go and spend the day at the Chapala Shrine."

It was a quirk of Buddha's that though he disapproved of "tanks and shrines" in general, he loved the tree-shrines sacred to the Yakshas, the tutelary genii of the tribes. He liked to sleep or meditate beside a Yaksha shrine when there was one handy.

The two old men spread their mats under the giant

lanterns of branches and creepers. Buddha said, "How delightful a spot is Vaisali, Ananda; and how charming is this shrine." They mused for a while.

Then Buddha spoke: "Ananda. As you know, whoever has mastered the four paths of *iddhi* may possibly— should he desire to do so—use them to prolong his life; to remain alive in the same birth for an aeon.

"Now, Ananda, I have mastered the four paths of *iddhi*."

Ananda did not reply. We can't guess why. Tradition says that Mara, the Evil One (who was hovering in the vicinity) had dulled his mind; or perhaps he was just old and tired and had fallen into a doze. It was obviously his duty to guess Buddha's thought, to realize his wish to remain alive for years, and to offer him the loving persuasion he required by responding eagerly: "Live, lord! Live on through the aeon, O Happy One. For the good and happiness of multitudes, live on!" But Ananda's ears were deaf to the Lord Buddha's broad hint, and he did not reply.

Buddha spoke again, explaining in distinct language that it was well within his powers to stay alive. Ananda still said nothing. For the third time Buddha delivered his hint, but to no avail, and finally he said sharply, "Leave me, Ananda, and do whatever you see fit."

Ananda heard this command, and he moved off to sit alone.

Now Mara appeared, the Evil One, grinning. "Lord, it is time! May you now attain Nirvana; let the Exalted One pass away."

Buddha replied, "No, Evil One. I shall not die. Not

until the monks and nuns have learned everything they have to learn by heart!"

"But this is done," said Mara.

"Yet I shall not die," Buddha said, "until they are able to teach others."

"But this is done!" insisted Mara.

"Still I shall not die until they are able to refute false doctrine."

"This is done, lord, done," said Mara impatiently.

And Buddha said, "I shall not die until this pure teaching of mine shall have become successful, widespread, and popular."

"All this is done!" cried Mara. "It is time for you to die!"

Buddha gazed serenely upon the Evil One. Mara began to gnash his teeth in sudden rage. He had just realized the trap that had been laid for him: he had been provoked into admitting that Buddha had succeeded in all that he had set out to do. As he fumed, Buddha said, "Calm yourself, Evil One. The death of the Truth-finder shall take place in good time. At the end of three months I shall pass away."

With this Mara had to be content, and he slunk off.

Buddha now sat in deep meditation. He schooled his mind to relinquish all need to live. Deliberately and consciously he emptied himself of every affection or joy in life, every regret for things undone, and he put away his doubts. He shook himself free of the world, and as he did so, the earth trembled.

Ananda came running in alarm. Buddha calmed him and made him sit down. Then he told him about his

The Sung Dynasty (960–1280 A.D.) was one of the
grand periods of Chinese art and was particularly noted for
fine portraits. The sculptor of this iron head has been careful to
show the narrow nose and strongly defined brow-ridge
of an Indian nobleman; and yet his Buddha still resembles a
Chinese Mandarin.

*Courtesy The Metropolitan Museum of Art*

encounter with the Evil One and that he would die in
three months' time. Ananda's mind cleared, his tongue
loosened, and he exclaimed in terror, "Lord! Remain during the aeon; live on for the good and happiness of multitudes! Lord, out of pity for the world, live on!"

Buddha told him, a bit severely, that his entreaties
were too late.

About February of the year 483 B.C., he collected his
monks together and proposed to them that they should
travel still northward into the country of the Mallas.
They went slowly, zigzagging between towns and villages where communities of monks and nuns lived, and
Buddha tirelessly delivered discourses, all memorable because they were a summing up of his teachings. "Keep
watch on your own hearts," he reiterated. "Share in
common." "Persevere in kindness of action, speech, and
thought." He spoke earnestly on the subject of accurate
reportage, explaining how the Doctrine had been arranged
as a check on false theories.

"You may hear a brother say, 'From the mouth of the
Blessed One himself have I heard this, from his own
mouth. It is the truth.' Or he may say, 'I have heard this
from the elders and leaders, versed in the truths,' or 'from
a sage holding the faith as handed down by tradition.'

"These words, monks, should be received neither with
praise nor treated with scorn. With neither praise nor
scorn, every syllable should be carefully understood and
then placed beside the Dharma and the Higher Doctrines
and the Rules and compared. If, when so compared, they
do not fit, you may come to the conclusion, 'The Blessed
One did not say this, it is not the truth, the Teaching

has been wrongly grasped by that brother.' "

He led them into the Malla country. There was a black-smith living near the border named Chunda, a man of low caste, but well-to-do. His father was the dancing master of the Malla nobles. They stopped at his mango grove, and Chunda asked them to do him the honor of taking a meal at his house. By silence, Buddha gave his consent.

The next morning he rose, robed himself, and taking his bowl went with his brethren to Chunda's house. Rice and cakes were prepared, and also a dish made with truffles, a sort of mushroom that grows underground and is found with difficulty by watching where the wild boars root. It was a delicate and rare food then, as it is now.

Buddha knew at once that there was something wrong with the truffle dish, and he said to Chunda, "Serve me the truffles. Give the others rice and cake." He had always taught that a monk must eat what is put before him, neither liking nor disliking; besides, he had already taken his leave of life.

When he had finished, he told Chunda, "Whatever truffles you have left, bury them in a hole. I know of no one in heaven or earth who can digest that dish, except the Truth-finder."

Flurried, but not alarmed by this command, Chunda obeyed. Then Buddha gave him thanks for his hospitality with a discourse. By the time he ended his talk, terrible pains had seized him, but he gave no sign of them. He said to Ananda, "Let us go on to Kusinara."

They traveled toward Kusinara, and after they had gone a way, Buddha told Ananda, "Fold, I pray you, a robe in four, and spread it out for me. I am weary and must rest."

He did not lie down, but sat in his accustomed posture of meditation, striving to calm with his mind the agonies of his body. After a while he said, "Fetch me some water, Ananda."

"Lord, I cannot," replied Ananda. "The wagons are going over the stream and it is muddied. Let's walk on, lord, a little way to the river Kakuttha which is clear, pleasant, cool, and transparent, and easy to get down into."

"Bring me some water, Ananda, I pray you."

"Lord, the wagons are even now crossing the stream and it is turbulent."

"Fetch water, Ananda." Ananda took Buddha's bowl to the stream and though the last of the wagons were still rumbling across, the water was clear as crystal.

The Blessed One drank and rested. A passing caravan stopped and its owner came toward him. He said his name was Pukkusa, and once, as a boy, he had known Alara Kalama, Buddha's old *guru*. He sat down for a chat and they exchanged reminiscences. Pukkusa, who had not pursued the saintly life but had gone into business, spoke with admiration of Alara who could sit in meditation totally unconscious of sound or sight even of five hundred carts going past his very nose. "How wonderful a thing it is and how marvelous," he said, "that those who have gone forth can pass their time in a state of mind so calm."

Buddha told him that there was one thing even more wonderful: to be totally unconscious of disturbances while outwardly fully conscious. But he did not explain that he was referring to himself at that moment, refusing to feel his fierce pains.

Before passing on, Pukkusa insisted on bringing from his caravan two princely robes made of cloth of gold, one for Buddha and the other for Ananda. It was not the sort of gift monks generally accepted, but Buddha allowed the robe to be placed around his shoulders. For the first time in years the cousins were arrayed like noble Sakyas. Ananda looked grand. But Buddha's exalted state of mind had brought luminosity to his golden skin. His visage was calm as a statue, and as he discoursed to Pukkusa, giving thanks, the gold of the garment dimmed. "How strange, lord," said Ananda when Buddha had finished speaking, "that on your body this cloth of gold loses its splendor."

"Yes, Ananda," said Buddha. "There are only two occasions when such a thing can happen: the night a Truth-finder becomes enlightened, and the night he dies."

Ananda was appalled. But Buddha bade him call the flock together so that they might move on. It was his wish to go to the Sala Grove at Kusinara, so-called for the famous twin sala trees that grew there, identical in size and shape. There was some shelter there too, a small monastery.

They crossed the river Kakuttha, where they bathed and drank, and again Buddha rested on the bank. Now his companions were aware of his dire condition and approaching death. They had remembered the truffles, and were furious with Chunda. Buddha said privately to Ananda, "It may be that someone will stir up remorse in Chunda. If that happens, check it. Say, 'It was a good thing for you, Chunda, and great merit, that the Truth-finder had his last meal by your alms.' Tell him I said so."

Presently he regained strength and they went on. They arrived at the Sala Grove. A bench had been built between the twin trees on which Ananda spread a folded robe for Buddha, and now at last he lay down on his right side with one leg resting on the other. By a freak, the sala trees were blooming out of season, swaying in the breeze from the Himalayas, and some blossoms fell on him. Ananda pointed out that Nature was doing Buddha honor, but Buddha said, "It is not by this that I am honored. It is by the brothers and sisters, the devout men and women, who continually honor the Dharma. This is homage."

There was a monk, an old attendant, standing in front of Buddha anxiously fanning him, and the Master commanded him with asperity to stand aside. Then he excused his brusque tone: "There are shades about me, Ananda, shades without number gathering in the Sala Grove; not only spirits of the air and heaven, but those created by earthly thought. And some do mourn, and weep, falling prostrate on the ground. But others are still and calm."

The monks waited and they watched. Occasionally they asked a question, and Buddha replied. Ananda said, "What shall we do with your remains, lord?"

"Treat me like a king," replied Buddha. He meant that he wished to be cremated. He gave explicit instructions: his body was to be wrapped in new cloth and then in cotton wool, and so on for many layers. It was to be placed in a coffin of iron and burned on a pyre. The coffin was then to be placed in a cairn at a crossroads where people could pass by it and leave flowers behind, remembering him and his Dharma.

Ananda was heavy with grief. He rose and went stumbling into the monastery where he supported himself against the lintel of the door weeping—weeping not only for his Master but for himself because he had never learned to be detached from worldly love. "Alas, I am still but a learner, one who has work to do. And the Master is about to pass away from me—he who is so kind."

Buddha missed him and sent for him. Ananda returned and sank to the ground beside his couch. "Enough, Ananda," said the sage. "Grieve not. Have I not told you often that it is in the very nature of things near and dear to us that we must divide ourselves from them, leave them; everything on earth, Ananda, contains within itself the seed of decay."

Then Ananda, after his years of being told to come and go, to walk and sit, to fetch and carry, and having to take second place to Aharats, heard himself immortalized as his dying master praised him.

"For a long time, Ananda, have you been near to me with acts and words and thoughts of love, kind and good, never varying, and beyond all measure. You have done well, Ananda.

"Monks! He is a clever man, Ananda, and a wise one. He knows exactly how to handle the people of every caste and quality who come to see me. And when they come, they are gladdened when they see Ananda, and they are rejoiced when he preaches the Dharma to them.

But when Ananda is silent, the company is uneasy.

"In this Ananda is like a king of kings. For when a king speaks, the courtiers are gladdened. And when he says nothing, they are ill at ease.

"Such are the wonderful and marvelous qualities of Ananda."

He fell silent, and Ananda mourned. He wished he could think of a way to persuade Buddha to live. He began to find fault with the Sala Grove. "You can't die here, lord, in this wattle-and-daub town in the middle of a jungle. There are grand cities—Rajagriha, Sravasti, Kosambi. Let the Blessed One die in one of them in the house of a wealthy noble or Brahmin."

Buddha tried to cheer him up by telling him that once, in ages past, Kusinara had been a grand town full of palaces and the clash of cymbals. Failing, he bade Ananda go to the head men of Kusinara and tell them that he was dying and wished to take leave of them. Sorrowfully, Ananda did as he was told.

The moon rose over the Sala Grove. The forest quickened with shadows. But they were not shades or spirits, they were Mallas, by the dozens and hundreds, from Kusinara and the countryside around, who had heard that the Lord Buddha was dying in their grove and who wished to see him. Ananda was desperate. The lord would have to spend his last hours greeting Mallas, he would die greeting Mallas. He wanted to turn them away, but Buddha told him to admit them.

Ananda compromised. He divided up the Mallas into families, and ushered them in groups past the bench where Buddha was lying, repeating only the name of the head of the family: "Lord, a Malla called So-and-so with his children, his wives, his servants, and his friends, humbly bows down at the feet of the Blessed One."

In this way, Buddha took his leave of the Mallas of Kusinara.

When all was quiet again, another guest arrived. He was a wandering ascetic named Subhadra who, upon learning the reason for the commotion at the Sala Grove, came himself to see Buddha. He said to Ananda, "I have heard that the Great Recluse is a rare man, but I have never properly understood his teaching. Oh, that I might be able to see him!"

"No, friend Subhadra. The Blessed One is weary."

But Buddha had heard this conversation, and he consented to see Subhadra. "He has come for knowledge, not to annoy me. And he will quickly understand what I have to say."

Subhadra the Wanderer sat down beside Buddha and with his first question asked if other famous teachers such as Mahavira understood the Truth, and if not, why not. Buddha said, "Enough! Let the matter rest there whether other teachers understand the Truth or do not understand it. Listen well! I am going to teach you the Dharma."

When he had finished Subhadra asked to be ordained into the Samgha.

It was Buddha's last discourse, last conversion, last ordainment. He was very weak now. He called Ananda close to him and said, "It may be, Ananda, that some of you may think, 'The word of the Master is ended, we have no Teacher any more.' But this is not so, Ananda. The

Dharma is there and the Rules. They are your Teacher."

He called his monks close to him. They came and sat in silent groups, their yellow robes silvered under the moon. "Brethren," said Buddha, "think well. If there is any doubt or misgiving in the mind of any one of you, inquire freely. Do not reproach yourselves afterward with the thought, 'Our Teacher was face to face with us, and we could not bring ourselves to ask a question.'"

They were silent. The Master urged them: "If out of reverence for your Teacher you put no question, then let one friend confide his question to another."

No whisper came from the brothers. Ananda said, "It seems, lord, wonderful and marvelous though it may be, that in this assembly of monks, no one has any doubt or misgiving."

"You have spoken out of faith, Ananda," said Buddha. "But I speak from knowledge: I know that not one monk here has doubt or misgiving."

It was a statement of pride.

Then Buddha said, "Brethren! Everything that has a beginning must have an end. Work out your salvation with diligence."

He put his head on his arm, lying quietly on his right side with one foot on the other. He passed into trance, and presently his light went out.

The monks huddled like nesting birds in the rain.

# *And in the End...*

*It is as when a man writes a letter by lamplight.*
*When he has done, he puts out the light; but the*
*writing is still there.*

DIGHA-NIKAYA

With Buddha's death, the senior member of the Samgha was the aged Kasyapa, the former fire worshiper whom Buddha had converted shortly after delivering his first sermon. This venerable monk now assumed leadership of the Order and presided over the cremation ceremony.

Of course, Buddha's remains were not treated as he wished. There was an undignified squabble about them among the tribes, all wanting a share. Even the handful of surviving Sakyas put in their claim, calling him "the pride of our race."

In the end the relics were divided into eight parts, and in the course of centuries they were further subdivided. Today, bits and pieces of Buddha are believed by the devout to be enshrined in many shrines and temples throughout the Far East.

In 1898, a gentleman named W. C. Peppé, who lived

close to the Nepalese frontier, was digging in his garden around an ancient stupa, or cairn, and he unearthed several stone vessels containing bones, cut stones, and pieces of gold leaf. Around the rim of one vessel runs an inscription whose meaning is not agreed upon by all scholars; still, it is generally thought to read in part: "This is the relic-treasury of the Lord Buddha of the Sakyas."

The reliquary reposes in the Calcutta Museum, and may be evidence, if any is needed, of the existence of a "historical Buddha."

It is exasperating that though the educated Brahmins and Kshatriyas who surrounded Buddha knew how to read and write, not one of them dreamed, so far as we know, of recording his words. It was simply not the custom. In the remote past, and even in Buddha's day, religious teachings were often "mysteries," taught only to a few intimate disciples who learned them by heart. When Buddha told Ananda that he had kept "no closed fist" on his Doctrine, he was distinguishing himself from other teachers who did. But so strong is habit and tradition that it did not occur to him to make his teachings available in writing.

Kasyapa, aware of the danger that the teachings might be corrupted by inexact repetition, called a Council of Aharats shortly after Buddha's death. They met in a cave in one of the hills above Rajagriha. The day they met there, one seat was left vacant: that of Ananda, who was not an Aharat. But he had sat up all night in deep trance striving to achieve supreme enlightenment. For once all of his brothers were on his side: they needed Ananda, not only because he had known Buddha more intimately than any of them, but also because they wanted to accuse him of everything that had gone wrong in the Samgha for the last forty years.

He appeared at the entrance of the cave, his face illumined. He had achieved Aharat-ship. The brothers led him to his place and pounced. His most important crime was in failing to persuade Buddha to stay alive; his next, the key role he had played in getting women admitted to the Samgha; then, he had once stepped on a robe of Buddha's while it was being sewn; and so on for a long time. In times of stress, it seems, even saints may need a scapegoat.

When Ananda had been dealt with, they turned to their main purpose. Between them they recalled everything that Buddha had said and done and taught, and to make certain that they knew it all exactly, they chanted in unison. They followed Upali in matters of doctrine; they followed Ananda in the matter of Buddha's discourses, conversations, and actions. For seven solid months they chanted. Presumably only a part of what they chanted has been preserved for us, but what we have got fills thousands of pages.

Just over a hundred years later, in 377 B.C. a Second Council was called, and again the teachings were checked against the best memories and chanted.

In the meanwhile, the world was changing. The political and social turbulence, the simmering tribal rivalries that Buddha had known in his lifetime, turned into chaos when Alexander the Great brought his armies into India.

This gave a chance to the ambitious kings of Magadha to unite the petty kingdoms of the north and northwest against the foreign invaders. In the late fourth century there arose a certain Chandragupta Maurya, a splendid organizer and leader, who not only delivered his country from the power of Alexander's satraps, but built an empire which extended over most of northern India.

It was Chandragupta's grandson, Asoka the Great, who became converted to Buddhism and made it the state religion of the Maurya Empire. In effect, Asoka was the St. Paul of Buddhism: not only did he exhort his own subjects to "follow the Good Law," but he sent missionaries far and wide across the lands and seas of the Far East. Their teachings made Buddhism one of the dominant religions of the world.

Asoka called a Third Council at Pataliputra in 247 B.C., almost two and a half centuries after Buddha's death, and once more the doctrine was rehearsed and solemnly chanted. When Asoka's son, Prince Mahendra, a monk of the Samgha, was sent as missionary to Ceylon, he took with him a sort of walking library: a band of reciting monks, all of whom knew the surviving texts by heart.

It is Mahendra's Ceylonese converts whom we must congratulate for first committing to writing, in the first century B.C., what we now know as the "Pali Canon," the earliest surviving Buddhist scriptures. The Canon is considered to be a reasonably accurate record of Buddha's life and teachings.

However, while generations of elders struggled to preserve the old traditions, other forces were at work on

Buddha. He was being made into a miraculous being. People were telling each other enchanting tales about him, especially of his early life. In the course of centuries, the figure of Buddha became something more than human, and as the religion spread, the Buddha-nature came to be worshiped in many forms and under many names.

This luxuriantly mythological style of Buddhism is called Mahayana, the Greater Vehicle, and it is followed by northern Buddhist countries such as Tibet, China, and Japan.

But southern Buddhist lands, such as Ceylon, Burma, and Thailand, continue to treasure the Theravada, the "Way of the Elders." In these lands the Pali texts are studied, and each Buddhist is required to have a personal understanding of Buddha the man and monk. It is here, in the Hinayana, or Little Vehicle school, that we find retained a sense of the "historical Buddha" as, for the most part, we have seen him in this book.

The first portion of this book, describing Buddha's life up to his appearance among the *gurus* of the Vindhya Mountains, is based chiefly on the *Lalitavistara,* a Sanskrit work of the second or third century A.D. It is a romantic and poetic account; in it, we can almost see a god in the making. The rest of the book, dealing with Buddha's work and character and events after he became a Teacher, is based on the books of the Pali Canon. The quotations at the chapter headings are from the Canon, except that which heads the chapter on Buddha's Enlightenment, paraphrasing the famous words of St. Paul.

All conversations and spoken words are from the Canon,

though they have been contracted and simplified, at the expense, I am afraid, of their archaic grandeur. But I hope that some readers will desire to look into the old texts, where they will see for themselves the splendor of the Chain of Causation expanding and then contracting into the Four Noble Truths; and have the pleasure of hearing Buddha say, "The Truth-finder does not live with full habit," instead of "I am not fat."

No doubt there will come some unimaginable day when the light of Asia will go out. The great stone images and the jeweled ones will have turned to dust and the gold-pinnacled temples will be ground under the earth. Not a person will be alive to remember that Gautama Buddha ever lived or to recite the Canon.

Buddhists do not dread this day, however. Their Teacher warned them of it, and he told them about his successor, Maitreya, who, when it is time for another Buddha-age to begin, will arise in the world "endowed with knowledge and right conduct, a knower of the worlds, incomparable, a teacher of gods and men; and he will proclaim and make known the Doctrine, lovely at the beginning, lovely in the middle, and lovely at the end."

At present Maitreya is a Bodhisattva sitting in the Heaven of Delight. He meditates upon the earth in time and space, and he has already chosen the conditions of his rebirth. His name means "friend": something all of us will always need.

# Bibliography

Brewster, E. H., *The Life of Gotama the Buddha* (from the Pali Canon). London, 1926.

Brown, Brian (ed.), *The Story of Buddha and Buddhism: His Life and Sayings*. Philadelphia, 1927.

Conze, Edward, *Buddhist Scriptures*. Penguin Books, 1959.

———, *Buddhism, Its Essence and Development*. Harper Torchbooks. New York, 1959.

Coomaraswamy, Ananda K., and Horners, I. B., *The Living Thoughts of Gotama the Buddha*. London, 1949.

Davids, T. W. Rhys, *Buddhism*. London, 1899.

*Digha-Nikaya, Dialogues of the Buddha* (Sacred Books of the Buddhists), trans. by Rhys Davids.

Hackin, J., and Maspero, Henri, *Asiatic Mythology*. New York, n.d.

*Jataka Tales*, Intro. and Notes by H. T. Francis and E. J. Thomas. Cambridge, 1916.

*Lalitavistara*, trans. by Rājendralala Mitra. Calcutta, 1882–86.

Lillie, Arthur, *The Popular Life of Buddha*. London, 1883.

*Majjhima-Nikaya, Further Dialogues of Buddha* (Sacred Books of the Buddhists), trans. by Lord Chalmers. Oxford, 1926–27.

Majumdar, R. C., Raychaudhuri, H. C., and Datta, Kalikinkar, *An Advanced History of India*. London, 1948.

Radhakrishnan, S., *Indian Philosophy*. London, 1923.

Saunders, Kenneth J., *The Story of Buddhism*. London, 1916.

———, *Gotama Buddha: A Biography*. London.

*Sutta-Nipata, Dialogues of Gautama Buddha* (Sacred Books of the Buddhists), trans. by Sir M. Coomaraswamy, 1874.

Thomas, E. J. (ed.), *Buddhist Scriptures*. London, 1913.

———, *The Life of Buddha as Legend and History*. London, 1927.

*Visakapuja*, Buddhist Association of Thailand. Bangkok, 1961.

Wagiswara, W. D. C., and Saunders, K. J., *The Buddha's Way of Virtue* (Dhammapada). London, 1912.

# Index